D1198406

CHRISTIANITY AND MANAGEMENT

HOW YOU CAN BECOME A SUCCESSFUL CHRISTIAN MANAGER THROUGH SERVANT LEADERSHIP!

Enjoy

Theodore H. Kittell

Theodore H. Kittell, PhD, JD, DLitt

Copyright © 2004 by Theodore H. Kittell

All rights reserved. No part of this book shall be reproduced or transmitted in any form or by any means, electronic, mechanical, magnetic, photographic including photocopying, recording or by any information storage and retrieval system, without prior written permission of the publisher. No patent liability is assumed with respect to the use of the information contained herein. Although every precaution has been taken in the preparation of this book, the publisher and author assume no responsibility for errors or omissions. Neither is any liability assumed for damages resulting from the use of the information contained herein.

ISBN 0-7414-1819-3

Scripture quotations are from the Contemporary English Version Bible; copyright, American Bible Society, 1995. Used with permission.

Comments welcomed by the author.

Theodore H. Kittell
PO Box 737, Dayton, TN, 37321
Email: ted@volstate.net
Fax: 423-775-9977

Published by:

INFI∞ITY
PUBLISHING.COM

519 West Lancaster Avenue
Haverford, PA 19041-1413
Info@buybooksontheweb.com
www.buybooksontheweb.com
Toll-free (877) BUY BOOK
Local Phone (610) 520-2500
Fax (610) 519-0261

Printed in the United States of America

Printed on Recycled Paper

Published November 2003

Dedications and Appreciation

I dedicate this handbook in memory of my father, Arthur C. Kittell, Sr. He often talked to me about business and management. I did not realize until years later that much of what he was telling me came from the Bible. I knew he read the Bible, but he rarely quoted it. He lived every day everything he learned from the Bible.

I also dedicate this handbook in memory of Ora B. Clark, my science teacher in high school. We had many discussions about passages in the Bible. He became my friend and confidant for the rest of his life. I feel he is still with me as my friend.

I offer my profound appreciation to my wife, Martha Hicks Kittell who has helped me with this handbook. Her expertise with English has helped me with many of the writings I have done over the years.

I also thank Dorothy Carter Rose for taking the time to proof read this manuscript. Her suggestions were most helpful.

Christianity and Management

Table of Contents.

PROLOGUE

The Love We Hold Back Is The Pain We Live With.

Ora B. Clark, 1951

This handbook is the product of many years of Bible study and my experiences as a manager. A few years ago I began to look for books on Christianity and Management. There is very little in print but there are two sources that are annotated for people in business. *Priority Profiles for Today* by Rev. Charles Stanley, Thomas Nelson Publishers, Nashville. *Business by the Book* by Larry Burkett, Thomas Nelson Publishers. These are two sources that can be used by a manager when they have specific problems. There is also *Jesus, CEO, Using Ancient Wisdom for Visionary Leadership* by Laurie Beth Jones, Hyperon Publishers, New York. This is an excellent book as a guide to communicating with and motivating people. I recommend that Christian managers read this book.

Management consultants including Warren Bennis, Peter Drucker, Tom Peters, Robert Greenleaf and Ken Blanchard used the term servant leadership suggesting that leaders move from toughness to tenderness and from controlling to serving. However, these men did not always give credit to the New Testament where servant leadership is described in Mark 10: 42-44, CEV and also in Luke 22: 24-27, CEV. Jesus Christ practiced the concept of servant leadership. More recently servant leadership was used by Mahatma Gandhi and Nelson Mandella. See Appendix 3 for other books on servant leadership.

This handbook covers many of the subjects that are found in many management texts. While I quote passages from the Bible, these are meant to support the practical conduct of Christian managers. As Laurie Beth Jones stated in her author's notes, *I view the Bible as the record of an intense love story between us and God, I* could not agree more.

My definition of a Christian manager is quite simple. A Christian manager is one who says he is a Christian. Christian management in many aspects is the same as secular management. What is different is the mental attitude and approach of Christian managers.

This handbook is intended to show Christian managers how the Bible supports many of the aspects of secular management, and how they can become successful as Christian managers using the servant leadership model. In the tumultuous world we live in and the dog eat dog managers that are present in the world of business with few if any ethical standards, the Christian manager will at times find it is difficult to be a servant leader. If he is to be true to this calling on the Lord and the gospels, the Christian Manager must persevere and manage with a strict code of ethics.

There are many Christian managers as well as secular managers that are inept and inadequate as managers. There are also very successful Christian managers and secular managers. A non Christian manager can use the servant style of management just as effectively as a Christian manager, if they choose to do so.

Chapter One

Introduction

Lord, what are your directions for me today?
I am waiting to hear the announcement,
This is your captain speaking!
I am ready and willing.
Give me orders and take charge of my life.
It's going to be a great day!
AMEN

Secular Versus Christian Management

Many Christian managers are finding conflict with the secular styles of management and their Christian beliefs. This handbook will focus on principles from the Bible in regard to managers and management. It will focus on leading people. The emphasis will be on the practical aspects of leadership and management and will follow the same topics found in most texts on secular management. The subject of anger in chapter eleven is included because this normal emotion can get managers in trouble.

There are many similarities between secular and Christian management, but there are also profound differences, particularly in regard to working with people. Is Christian management only secular management theories and techniques used by people who call themselves Christian? Are Christian managers people that hold themselves to a higher level of ethics? Or do Christian managers apply the principles of servant management, which conforms to Biblical principles? These questions are critical when addressing the critical elements such as organizational structure and authority within a particular business.

The secular organization has the profit motive at its core. A Christian manager should operate with a people motive related to customer and employee satisfaction. Profit is a natural result of a more efficient organization. Historically Christian managers have used secular management philosophy and principles. The secular approach is humanistic and materialistic. The authority and power positions are often used to manipulate and control people. My sincere hope and prayer are that you and your organization will be more satisfied with your work and more productive as a result of reading this handbook.

Secular Definition of Management.

The secular definition of management is, getting work done through others. This gives managers the right to control and exploit those under them.

But Jesus called the disciples together and said; You know that foreign rulers like to order their people around, and their great leaders have full power over everyone they rule. But don't act like them. If you want to be great, you must be the servant of all the others, and if you want to be first, you must be the slave of all the rest. The Son of man did not come to be a slave master, but a slave who will give his life to rescue many people, Matt. 20:25-28, CEV.

This passage from Matthew shows a marked contrast between the secular philosophy of management and Jesus Christ's philosophy of management. The Christian manager is to serve those under him by helping them to achieve the most they can. The higher up in an organization a Christian manager goes, the more he has to serve.

The authoritarian approach to management stimulates workers discontent, frustration and negative attitudes toward managers. When questioned responses workers give are: Managers see people just as tools to get the work done; I'm paid to work not to think; I do the work, but the boss gets the credit; They are not interested in me as a person, but only what I can do for them.

Jesus knew the secular approach to management and leadership had relational problems resulting in poor productivity. He told his disciples not to pattern their lives using the secular philosophy of management, and not to use authority and power to control people and pressure them to produce.

Secular management techniques and skills get people to change so you can get more out of employees thus more profit. The question is, are employees resources to be maximized or are employees the business's greatest asset to be facilitated in ways that allow them to perform at their best?

God Is In Control.

The big question is one of control. If a manager does not believe that employees are basically and intrinsically good, he must exert control to gain maximum utility from the investment in people. A Christian managers philosophy is based on the fundamental idea that God is in control. God knows best how to get people to motivate themselves in order to do the best work. It is man's purpose to serve others in such a way as to remove obstacles that lie between them and their complete submission to God. Is the secular and Christian approach incompatible? Certainly not!

God runs the universe, and His principles are sufficient to serve as foundational practices to operate a business. Christian managers need to learn to apply God's principles to an organization. This goes well beyond ethical behavior. It must consider the Christian assumptions of employee relationships as well the motive and purpose of the organization.

Biblical Definition of Management.

The biblical approach to management can be defined as management meeting the needs of people as they work at accomplishing their jobs. A manager will find by using this approach to management the people will look forward to their work. In return the managers' needs will be met. For a description of what the Christian managers attitude should be read Philippians 2: 1-8 CEV.

Your attitude should be the kind that was shown by Jesus throughout his life as a man. He did not demand and cling to His right as the Son of God. He laid aside his mighty powers and took the disguise of a slave and became like man. Jesus was called the King of the Jews. However, his conduct was that of a common man except when he was performing miracles.

Training People.

Another important aspect of Christian management is to train people. If you train and serve people, the sky is the limit as to what they can become as long as they are doing the will of God. We are familiar with the story of the Tower of Babel, where the people united to build a tower to reach to the heavens. This was not the will of God and the Lord scattered the people over the earth and confused their language so they could not understand each other. This story of the Tower of Babel gives four premises for a successful organization.

Commitment to work on a goal, Gen. 11: 3-4, CEV.

Unity among the people, Gen. 11:6, CEV.

Effective communication, Gen. 11:1,6, CEV.

Doing the will of God, Gen. 11:7-9, CEV.

The last premise shows the people who building the Tower of Babel were not doing the will of God. Organizations using these four premises will be successful. When people are committed to work on a goal, have unity, and have good communication, nothing is impossible for them to achieve. Unless God stops them, they will accomplish what they set out to do. Most organizational problems fall into three basic categories.

- Lack of commitment to a clearly defined goal.
- Lack of being united within and between departments.
- Poor communication.

In most cases, poor communication causes the other two problems. By learning the skill of identifying the basic cause of a problem the manager will be able to lead his people to solve the problem.

Secular Field of Management.

Approximately fifty years ago there was a split in management training from an academic perspective. One group approached the teaching of management with the perception of managers as rational technicians, who apply the principles of management science in the workplace. The other group approached the teaching of management as viewing managers as craftsmen who practice an art that cannot be captured by scientific principles. This split has had profound impact on the teaching of management in our Colleges and Schools of Business.

It would help the Christian manager to become familiar with these two approaches to management theory. How you work with other managers and top management can be helped to know which approach the various managers are using. This will give the Christian manager considerable insight in how to work with other managers. You will at times be working with other managers that may be in conflict because of the different approaches to management theory.

You will notice as you read this handbook that I have tried to blend the scientific management approach and the art of management approach when discussing secular management theory. The Christian approach to management is for the most part the art of management..

Chapter Two

Leadership and Ethics

Leadership Style.

Leadership style can exert an influence on how organizations flourish and on their productivity. See Ezekiel 34 which gives us an example of how leadership style can impact people and their productivity. The leader or manager should not exploit those who work for him. The effective Christian manager uses his position to serve the needs of others, not just force them to serve his needs. The Christian manager should serve willingly and eagerly.

Just as the shepherds watch over their sheep, you must watch over everyone God has placed in your care. Let it be something you want to do, instead of something merely to make money, 1 Peter 5: 2, CEV.

The Christian manager should exhibit such a spirit of serving that people will willingly follow. Note in Ezekiel 34 that the excessive use of authority and failure to meet people's needs drive them away. The New Testament tells us not to dominate those under us.

Don't be bossy to those people who are in your care, but set an example for them, 1 Peter 5: 3, CEV.

If you want them to serve and obey you, then you should do what they ask today. Tell them you will make their work easier, 1 Kings 12: 7, CEV.

Secular Styles of Management

We will examine in this chapter the four styles of management used by secular managers and the Christian style of servant management as well as the secular style of servant management. It is generally accepted in management texts that there are four basic styles of leadership; dictatorial, authoritative, consultative and participative.

Dictatorial Style.

The first is called dictatorial because the manager acts like a dictator. He makes all the decisions concerning what, when, where and how his people do the work. If his instructions are not carried out, his people will be disciplined.

An example of this style is where King Nebuchandnezzar had a dream and commanded his wise men to tell him what the dream was and to explain it. When they could not, he became furious and told them they would be killed if they could not explain it. See Daniel 2: 1-13, CEV.

The dictatorial manager has the following traits. He keeps all decision-making power to himself. He is usually unrealistic in his work demands and will ask his people to do the impossible. He frequently uses excessive discipline and punishment for those who do not carry out his instructions. He does not allow people to question his decisions or authority.

Authoritative Style.

Few managers consistently operate from a dictatorial style. At times they will adopt the authoritative style.

Saul, Israel's first King, provides an illustration of an authoritative leader in action. Saul was a very decisive leader. He used his authority to motivate people to follow him into battle. See 1 Sam. 11, CEV. However, he overstepped his authority by performing priestly sacrifices. See 1 Sam. 13, CEV. His quick decisions and pride almost caused the death of his son Jonathan. See 1 Sam. 14, CEV.

The authoritative leader or manager has the following characteristics. He seldom lets others make decisions. He feels he is the most qualified. He considers his views to be the most valid. He is frequently critical of opinions and decisions that differ from his opinions and decisions. Frequently he does not have confidence in other peoples abilities. He rarely gives his employees recognition for a job well done.

He will use other people's ideas only if he agrees with them. He will be offended if other people disagree with his point of view. He frequently uses other people for his own benefit and is action-oriented. He is highly competitive. The authoritative manager's main weakness is his failure to recognize the skills and abilities of his people. His strength is his ability to produce action when it is needed.

Consultative Style

The consultative style of leadership focuses on using the skills and ideas of others in formulating plans and making decisions. Usually the consultative leader retains the final decision-making power. However, he does not make major decisions without consulting with those affected by his decisions.

As the church grew in the early centuries, some people's needs were not met. See Acts 6: 1-7, CEV. This is also a problem that growing churches have today. When the Grecian Jews pointed out that some of their widows were being neglected, the apostles told them to choose seven men who would be appointed to serve the widow's needs. This passage in Acts clearly shows the consultative style of leadership. The seven people work on the solution to the problems the widows are having.

The consultative style manager focuses on building a team. The manager usually reserves the right to make the final decision. The manager has time to work on other things while the team gathers information to solve the problem. This is a major strength of consultative leadership style.

The consultative manager does the following. He asks for input from subordinates on a regular basis. He never makes decisions without the input from those affected by the decision. He works at providing proper recognition to those working on the decision and is willing to delegate certain decision-making power, but he retains veto authority. He attempts to weigh all alternatives suggested before making a decision and then explains why certain ideas were not used.

Keep in mind that the consultative manager will generally act the way described, but there are times that he may not act in this manner. The consultative manager is a thoughtful manager and cares for the needs of his people to a great extent.

Participative Style.

The participative style of leadership is a unique leadership style. Many managers feel uncomfortable using this style. In the participative style the manager will give most of his authority to the team. The manager may retain some of his authority and is the team leader.

The participative style of management has the following traits. Members of the team are equal with the manager in terms of input and ideas. Everyone's ideas are considered. The manager is the facilitator and coach for the team. The manager usually accepts the team's ideas, even when they disagree with his. The manager focuses on stimulating creativity and innovation within the team.

Use of the Management Styles.

Use of the dictatorial style is appropriate: during extreme emergencies or crises when people's life and property are at stake. You want your people to act quickly during this time. You do not have the time to use one of the other styles. The dictatorial style is also appropriate when severe disciplinary action is needed, but it must be handled very carefully. This leadership style should be used only on a temporary basis.

Use the authoritative style when the people you are working with are inexperienced and need training. It is also appropriate when immediate action is needed. This leadership style should be phased out as your team becomes trained and capable of working with loose control by the manager.

Use the consultative style when conducting ongoing planning for the team. Use this style also when creative problem solving is needed, in training people to assume leadership responsibilities and when performing daily routine functions and tasks.

Use of the participative style is appropriate as people become competent in performing their routine tasks and responsibilities; when doing planning sessions; during organizational evaluation sessions; when you need to motivate qualified people who tend to become stifled in their routine tasks and assignments and any time there is a need for creative and innovative ideas.

There are short term and long-term effects of the various manager styles. Over a short span of time, the authoritative style may produce the greatest results. If this style is used excessively, it will decrease productivity. The participative style tends to be unproductive over a short period of time. However, the longer this style is used, it becomes more productive. The manager should not be discouraged by a drop in productivity as he changes to this style.

Servant Leadership

The apostles got into an argument about which one of them was the greatest. So Jesus told them:

> *Foreign kings order their people around, an powerful rulers Call themselves everyone's friend. But don't be like them. The most important one of you should be like the least important and your leader should be like a servant. Who do people think is the greatest, a person who is served or one who serves others? Isn't it the one who serves others? But I have been with you as a servant,* Luke 22: 24-27, CEV.

Greatness in leadership is giving oneself in service to others, not compelling others to serve the leader.

The Biblical model of leadership refers to the leader as a servant. This manager was one who nurtured, mentored and was an example of integrity. Contemporary authors have written about the servant leadership style of management. Leadership that was based on command, control, rank, and dominance appeared to be effective in the short run, while servant leadership is the basis for long term success.

Servant leadership includes trust, mutual care and concern, worker empowerment and loyalty. Contemporary authors do not know or choose not to give credit to the Biblical foundations for servant leadership. One of them has held himself out to have coined the new term of servant leadership. While in fact this style of leadership has been utilized over the centuries by great leaders, and indeed by Jesus Christ.

To determine your leadership style, look at the way you use authority. Do you delegate or make most of the decisions yourself? Your leadership style influences how you work with people. The more authoritative you are the less you will be willing to use the talents of your people. The more you use authority the more you will keep yourself separate from your workers. With the less authority you use, you will be working with people not people working for you.

By not delegating communication will be from the top management down through the chain of command to the workers. As the workers are given more authority, communication will be a two way process. It will be from the top down to the workers and from the workers to top management. Managers will ask workers for input instead of just giving instructions.

The manager should keep in mind that the leader style used can have a major role in an organization's productivity. The manager should also remember that his job is to serve the work related needs of those under him. Three key points greatly influence leader style.

- How you use authority.
- How you view people resources.
- How you relate to people.

Ethics.

I have included ethics in this chapter dealing with leadership. Appropriate ethical conduct and actions is closely integrated with leadership. The ethical conduct of the leader is of paramount importance for an organization both within the organization and with outside relationships. If the leader's conduct is ethical this will carry over to the workers in an organization.

An ethical person is one who is moral, virtuous, principled, honest, upright, decent, honorable, conscientious, righteous, right-minded, right thinking, upstanding, just and scrupulous. Another way of thinking of ethics is to use the word goodness which is defined as a person who has virtue, morality, integrity, honesty, righteousness uprightness, and probity, and righteousness. These definitions can apply to anyone.

Ethics can be defined for a particular business or profession. Most professions have ethics requirements. These ethics statements are what I choose to refer to as situational ethics standards. They are specific to the profession or business concerned. As the situation changes for the profession the ethics statements are changed. This can be contrasted to what I call true ethics standards. These are ethics that do not change with the passage of time. An example would be the ten commandments. See Ex. 20: 1-17. Even the commandment, *You should not kill* has been turned into a situational ethics statement. This commandment is now *You shall not kill except in time of war and when a person is executed for a crime he has committed.*

Many professions have ethics codes and in some instances these codes have been given the authority of law. An example would be the Ethics Code for the Practice of Law. If it is not followed, after a hearing, the attorney in question can lose his license to practice law or be put on probation. A Business Code of Ethics for board members has the effect of law due to common law decisions by the courts. Many who serve on boards are not aware there is a code of ethics where they can be held accountable for their actions in a court of law.

A biblical reference to ethics/morality is Acts 24:16, CEV.

Because I am sure, I try best to have a clear conscience in what ever I do for God or for people.

This is just one reference; others are as follows: Math. 5: 1-12, CEV; Tim. 3: 10-17; CEV, Tit. 2: 11-15, CEV; Prov. 22: 1, CEV; Luke 6: 1, CEV. You will not find in the Bible the word ethics. However, there are many passages in the Bible that you will know when it is about ethics/morality. To be ethical you must live your life by using the definitions given for ethics and for goodness. Another guide for the Christian manager is the golden rule. *Do unto others as you would have them do unto you.*

The Christian manager may be asked to do things that will conflict with his ethics and morality. This can even be to the point of losing his job if he does not comply. You will have to decide what you are going to do.

Chapter Three

Planning:
Organizational and Personal

Before starting the planning process, recognize that God has a plan for each of you and your organization. Some Christians will question that God has a plan for them. We have the free will to determine our own plan. That is true, but God in his wisdom knows what your plan will be. Recognize that God is the source of power to achieve your plan.

Most secular texts on management start with planning as the first subject, which is the base or foundation of successful management. Planning is the foundation of Christian management as well. Without planning, things just happen. Lack of proper planning puts people on the defense instead of the offense. Too much time will be spent working with problems that just happen.

The Bible and Planning.

The Bible has a lot to say about planning. It provides many principles concerning how the planning should be done. Planning consists of identifying the following items.

- The overall purpose of a project.

- What is to be done.

- The sequence of events to carry out the project.

- What is needed to accomplish the project.

If any of these elements are not done, plans will have little chance of success.

God, Plan and Purpose.

A Christian manager starts with the realization that God has a plan and a purpose. With the freewill God has given us, we must make our own plans. When we make a plan that feels right in our heart, we are at one with God.

> We make our own plans, but the Lord decides where we will go, Prov. 16:9, CEV.

> The Lord said, I will bless you with a future filled with hope, a future of success, not of suffering, Jer. 29:11, CEV.

> You said to me, I will point out the road that you should follow. I will be your teacher and watch over you, Ps. 32:8, CEV.

Share the Work.

Because God does have plans some people use this as an excuse not to plan. If God is in control, why plan? Some Christian managers are the opposite. They plan out every detail and think they must produce the results. They want to do it all. Paul said,

I planted the seeds, Apollos watered it, but God made them sprout and grow, 1 Cor. 3:6, CEV.

This passage tells us we must share the work.

The Christian manager must realize his job is to determine the actions God wants him to take and trust God for the results.

We may make a lot of plans, but the Lord will do what He has decided, Prov. 19:21, CEV.

These two scripture verses are easy to read, but hard to follow. How will we know what God has decided? We will do the planning and choose an alternative. The only way to know if it is what God has decided, is if it feels right in your heart. How will you know it is right in you heart? If everything feels all right with you and you have no doubts is how some people know it is right in their heart. As you progress and become experienced you will know when something is right in your heart.

Purpose.

The first part of the planning definition concerns the purpose. This is where planning should begin. The purpose deals with the question why. Why is this important? Why should I be involved? Why do we need to get this done? Why should this be top priority? Defining a purpose motivates people to get behind a cause. Jesus always recruited people to a cause or a purpose, not to a job or a plan. He assigned tasks only after people had joined His cause.

> *Jesus said to them, Come with me, I will teach you how to bring in people instead of fish,* Matt. 4:19, CEV.

Jesus ended his ministry by sharing some of the details of how his purpose was to be achieved.

> *Then he told them: Go and preach the good news to everyone in the world,* Mark 16:15, CEV.

An example of purpose is when God explained the purpose when he asked Noah to build an ark for his family and the animals. He answered Noah's questions about why. See Gen. 6:1-22, CEV. This principle of asking why is seen throughout the Bible. Unfortunately the question of why is often overlooked when we are doing planning.

Planning is difficult work. It is important to begin the planning process by identifying the overall purpose of the project. A strong sense of purpose helps develop the conviction and commitment needed for the work of planning. Too many planning meetings serve little purpose. Every planning meeting should begin with prayer and by answering the question, WHY ARE WE DOING THIS? If we cannot answer this question why we should take the time to find out why. Putting the project aside and coming back to it later sometimes helps.

Vision

Have a vision of the completed plan. This mental picture of the plan stimulates action, innovation and creativity. A vision provides people with the will to motivate themselves. It helps to create group unity and personal conviction.

Measurable Objectives.

Next one will need to have measurable objectives. A measurable objective will tell exactly what will be accomplished and when it will be accomplished. The king in regard to rebuilding of Jerusalem asked Nehemiah.

What is it you want and how long will your journey take? See Neh.2:4-6,CEV.

Nehemiah with his reply had measurable objectives for the rebuilding of Jerusalem.

If there are no measurable objectives how will one evaluate performance of the plan? Measurable objectives give meaning to the plan. Without measurable objectives, people tend to talk and plan in generalities. They will often usually not know when they have arrived at the conclusion of their plan without measurable objectives.

Measurable objectives focus on what God wants us to do. One will know what to pray for if one has this kind of objectives. One could pray for God to bless the business. It may be difficult to know when and if he has answered your prayers. With measurable objectives our prayers can focus on what we want God to help us with. We will know what we want to accomplish and when we expect it to be done.

A good objective should always be one that can be accomplished. If people realize it is impossible to accomplish a project in the time allotted, they become frustrated and tend to lose interest. Objectives should be realistic. At times a project may be possible to do but it may not be realistic. Objectives must be realistic and accomplishable. Each objective must be compatible with other organizational goals. If not compatible, they may conflict with other goals they will not contribute to a common purpose.

Good objectives are always motivational and will stimulate interest and commitment. They will provide the spark that ignites people to action. If people don't want to be involved with an objective, it will have little chance to succeed. Earlier it was stated that the purpose answers questions about why the plan is important. Objectives explain what is to be achieved and when. We now move to how the plan is to be accomplished.

People Participation.

Participation by all people involved is the key to developing good activities and tasks. People who carry out a task are the ones knowledgeable about how it can be done. Participation gives people ownership of the project. If not part of developing the activities and tasks, they often lack the motivation and conviction to see that it succeeds. Innovation and creativity can keep people from becoming stagnant in their work. People should be encouraged to find new and improved ways of performing even routine tasks.

Right Sequence.

Once the tasks or activities have been identified, they need to be placed in the right sequence of accomplishment. One has to be certain that each task is done at the right time. Doing a task at the wrong time can be devastating to a project. There are excellent computer programs that assist in the development of a time line for all the various activities.

Resources Needed.

One will have to determine what resources are needed to achieve the plan. Jesus pointed out that knowing the resources needed is essential to the completion of a plan.

Suppose you wanted to build a tower. What is the first thing you would do? Won't you sit down and figure how much it will cost and is there enough money to pay for it, Luke 14:28, CEV.

What will a king do if he has only ten thousand soldiers to defend himself against a king who is about to attack him with twenty thousand soldiers? Before he goes out to battle won't he first sit down and decide if he can win? Luke 14:31, CEV.

Resource planning is a major and important part of the planning process. The sequence of activities will impact the type of resources needed and when they will be needed. Key factors to be considered are: people, space, equipment, supplies, time and money.

Usually people are the most important and valuable resource for plans to succeed. When considering the people needed, the following questions should be asked. What type of skills, gifts, and abilities are needed for the activities or tasks? Do we have people in our organization with the skills needed? If we have to go outside our organization to find people with the skills needed, how shall we recruit them?

What type of facilities or building space do we need? Often this is overlooked in the planning process. Without adequate space, the project may fail. What type of equipment is needed and is it available? It is important to place the equipment needed in the right time sequence to know when and where this equipment will be needed. What type of supplies will be needed and how much? Adequate supplies must be available when needed.

How much time will be required to prepare for and execute each activity? This will determine how much time it will take to accomplish the project. How much money will be needed and when? This will be determined by the number of people, the equipment and supplies that will be needed and when they will be needed. At the same time, the amount of money available may determine what can be done. Sometimes projects can be adjusted by being changed or by stretching the time out for the project completion. At times you will do as much as you can on a project until the money runs out, then continue later.

Read the Bible.

An example of a plan would be David's instructions to the people and to Solomon to build the temple, See 1 Ch. 28:1-21, CEV. God looks at things from a long-range perspective. Joshua became the leader of Israel upon the death of Moses. The Lord speaking to Joshua said;

> Never stop reading the Book of the Law. He gave you. day and night you must think about what it says, Josh.1: 6-8, CEV.

Personal Planning.

Most people do some planning in a vague general way. I recommend very strongly that you write a five-year plan for yourself. Write it out year one, two, three, four and five. Do not make your plan in generalities, be very specific. For example you may put in your plan to buy a house. Be very specific and spell out what you want your new home to be like. Put in detail everything you want. Put in year one, the items you think you might accomplish the easiest. Include your church in the plan; for example, the amount one is going to tithe.

Things you have no control over will happen. An example would be an illness. These things only delay items in your plan. Be concerned only with things you can change. One can redo the plan whenever he wants too, but it should be done at least once a year. Have your plan be an active document. At the end of the first year, do your five-year plan over. Drop a year and add a year. The items that did not get done, if you still want them in the plan, move to the new plan. Some items may no longer be important to you. If so delete them from your plan.

By having a specific five-year personal plan, you will know what you want. You will know what specific items to put in your prayers. You will see that many of the items put in your plan become a self-fulfilling prophecy. Without a plan you probably will just drift through life. You probably plan more that you realize. You just don't put it in writing. By putting it in writing it will improve your chances that your plan will be accomplished.

It is easy to put off doing a personal plan in writing. If you will definitely take the time you will be rewarded. You will find as you rewrite your plan that it will get easier and you will become very good at personal planning as well as organizational planning. One method to use is set a time period, say an hour. When that hour is up, stop and come back to it with a second and subsequent time periods until you finish your plan. Look at your plan frequently and see where you are and whether it will have to be revised.

Chapter Four

The Work Environment

There is not much use of a biblical philosophy of management unless that philosophy of management is put to use in one's daily work.

> Obey God's message! Don't fool yourselves by just listening to it, James 1: 22, CEV.

For years we have been aware of the influence the work environment has on productivity. The manager is responsible for his groups' work environment. The managers' response to the groups' needs and his attitude toward people and their work are very important. The environment is also conditioned by the manager's use of authority, his response to mistakes and failures, and his willingness to give the team proper credit for its accomplishments.

Trust Relationships.

The Christian manager who wants to tap the unlimited creative potential of people must create a trust relationship with his group. To do so he must give appropriate decision-making power to all individuals in his group. These elements must be carried out consistently since they interlock to create a trust relationship. There is little value for a manager to demonstrate he trusts his people if he is unwilling to let them make appropriate decisions. A manager must be willing to turn mistakes and failures into learning experiences. If he does not, he will find his people are reluctant to make decisions when they are told to make decisions.

Trust is the most important element to develop to maintain a productive work environment. Trust brings about security and confidence. These are essential to innovation and creativity. Mistrust produces frustration, insecurity and fear. One cannot do his best working for a boss he cannot depend upon.

Trust begins with the manager. The manager must be willing to demonstrate trust if the people are to be trustworthy. Trust builds confidence and will stimulate production. Innovation involves risk. People who cannot trust their managers will never take the risks inherent with change, innovation and creativity. Mistrust breed's stagnation. Jesus Christ was the best manager the world has ever seen. He created a work environment for those He trained which allowed them to start the church. The manager who wants to create an effective organization should pattern it after the principles used by Christ.

Decision-Making Defined.

Decision-making is the right to determine what action will be taken. Delegation is important to demonstrate trust. Giving decision-making power to another person is the ultimate expression of trust. Jesus said to his disciples;

> *To preach the good news to every one in the world,* Mark 16:15, CEV.

Jesus stated the goal, but He gave the disciples the decision-making power about how the goal was to be accomplished.

Fear of Failure.

Fear of failure is one of the reasons why managers do not give decision-making power to other individuals. To create a productive environment a manager must be able to accept the risk of a certain amount of failures. When a failure happens the manager must turn it into a positive learning experience for his people. Fear is one of man's worst enemies. The parable of the talents is an example of fear of failure.

> *The servant who had been given one thousand talents came in and said, Sir, I know that you are hard to get along with. You harvest what you don't plant and gather crops where you have not scattered seed.*

I was frightened and went out an hid your money in the ground. Here is every single coin, Matt. 25: 24-25, CEV.

The servant's fear caused him to do nothing with the talents, thus he produced nothing. However, failure can be a positive learning experience. Anyone can criticize a person for a failure, but effective managers work with their people to turn their mistakes into positive learning experiences. This may be difficult to do, but with experience a manager will get better at helping his people. We all have probably known fear of failure. At times we have had a failure. We must learn to cope with failure, because sometimes we will fail.

Risk Definition.

Risk can be defined as exposing yourself to the possibility of loss or harm. What is so terrible about making mistakes? We learn from our mistakes. Intolerance of mistakes is what makes people not want to take risks. Fear of failure reduces the willingness to take risks.

The Christian manager who wants a highly productive work environment must promote innovation and change and be willing to live with the risk. People must be permitted to make mistakes, or even to fail. Effective managers will use the mistakes to teach his people in a positive manner.

When mistakes have been made the manager should meet with those involved. You will work with the persons involved to clarify what should have been done and what needs to be done to correct the mistake. If possible the persons who failed should correct the situation. The Christian manager should keep in mind that his job is to meet the work related needs of those he works with.

The manager should determine if he contributed to the failure by not meeting individual needs. Ask those involved if any aspect of the failure was the result of work related needs not being met. This shows the manager is open to accept part of the blame. If a manager tries to work this out himself, it will let people know they are not to be trusted or are not capable of correcting the problem. Their self-confidence will be undermined.

The manager has the opportunity to use the creativity of those involved to correct the problem as a learning experience. Using these processes Jesus was able to turn peoples mistakes and failures into a positive learning experience. Even though the disciples failed repeatedly, Jesus continued to give them the task of ministering to people. Jesus allowed His disciples to fail, to learn from the experience, and to try again. See Matt. 17: 14-21, CEV.

Being given the opportunity to correct your mistakes can be one of life's best teachers. When handled improperly by the manager failure can completely destroy an individual's self image, motivation and productivity.

Give Recognition.

Throughout the Bible, God emphasizes the importance of giving recognition to those who deserve it. This is shown in the Parable of the Talents.

> The servants who had made a profit with the coins the master had given them were told they had done very well. The master told them they would be put in charge of much more. The master was proud of them and told them so. See Matt. 25:14-23, CEV.

Recognize people you work with and demonstrate that you need to appreciate people's contributions. Giving recognition helps meet that need. Recognition motivates people to do their best. When their needs are fulfilled, the manager's needs will be fulfilled.

Management By Walking Around.

A technique that has worked well is management by walking around. You get out of your office and walk around your whole facility. When you walk around the facility, you will get to know people and will become familiar with their names. When they get used to you coming around, they will begin to give you information that you probably cannot get anywhere else. If you have more than one shift, be sure you walk around on all shifts.

A second technique is simple and takes very little time. Whenever you see someone doing a good job, tell him or her so. Later write them a short note of thanks. I have lost track of the number of times I have been thanked or it has gotten back to me through the grapevine that employees treasured these notes. People need to be needed. Often it takes very little for a person to feel he is needed.

Chapter Five

People, Things and Ideas

Basic Categories.

I frequently tell my students that if it were not for people, management would be an easy job. People are an organization's most valuable resource. In both Christian and secular organizations, this value is frequently overlooked.

Management actions may be reduced to three basic categories. These categories are the management of people, things and ideas. Unfortunately too many managers put people in the things category. It generally is easier to manage things than people and ideas. The management of things is working with tangibles, while ideas are working with intangibles. Working with people is a blend of both tangible and intangible.

Things include budgets, facilities, equipment and supplies. Things in most cases are easily controlled and can be accounted for. Things can be easily bought and sold. Most things can be easily stored until they are needed.

On the other hand, ideas can't be seen. They can be hard to evaluate and are often hard to explain. Ideas can be too easily ignored and can exist without managers being aware of them. Ideas are the most difficult to control. Ideas can exist as part of an organization and can be recognized as such. They can also exist independently of the organization, or in spite of the organization. Most employee grapevines involve ideas that grow and change as they are passed from employee to employee.

People at times can be difficult to work with. Until the 1980's the management training concept was to treat all employees the same. Although many managers still try to do this, managers are now taught that people are not the same. Employees were told to leave their personal problems outside the front door. You do not have to work with employees very long before you realize they bring their personal problems to work with them. One of the keys to being a successful manager is how well you work with the employees without taking their personal problems on your back.

Ideas.

All organizations and the projects they deal with start out as an idea in someone's mind. A manager must make the management of ideas as his top priority. What an organization will be tomorrow depends on how well it manages people and ideas today. One error many managers make is they think of themselves as the only source for ideas. They view their people as things to be used to get current work done. A manager is short changing himself if he finds himself giving more attention to buildings, budgets, and equipment than he does to people and ideas.

Creativity.

Creativity can be defined as the making of something new, or the rearranging of something old. Using this definition, God and man are the only sources of creativity. The creativity of the human mind is probably infinite.

God also said, Now we will make humans and they will be like us. So God created humans to be like himself, He made man and woman, Gen. 1: 26-27, CEV.

Being made like God, man has phenomenal creative ability. All people are creative if you will let them be. Creativity is not a gift of talent possessed by a special few. People do not need special training to be creative. They do not have to exert special effort. Creativity is a natural product of man's thinking processes. People will be as creative as their managers will let them. Unfortunately many managers fail to provide opportunities to be creative. This is tragic since tapping into human creativity is the most effective means of increasing individual and organizational productivity.

God expects the abilities and creativ individuals to be utilized. When an indiv makes a contribution, he should be g recognition for his effort. The Chris manager should encourage his people to their abilities and creativity. As this occurs Christian manager must give credit recognition to those responsible for ma improvements.

Creativity can find new and better way accomplishing a task. Progress improvement is stimulated by creativity, wl costs nothing. It is there to be used. Not to the creativity available is losing the source answers to problems.

Every Christian manager should concerned about making his organization productive as possible. He should keep in m that God has given people unlimited creat ability for innovation and problem solving. T Christian manager should focus on putti people's creativity to work as a means increasing productivity. Creativity fin solutions to organizational problems. There is solution for every problem. Get creative ide and proposals from the people you work with.

People Need To Be Needed.

One should find ways to tell people the are needed. People are full of ideas ar solutions to problems. People definitely want t

ontribute. When people contribute they feel needed. A good Christian manager makes sure his group has an opportunity to utilize their creativity. However many managers tell their people; follow me you can have all the jobs I don't want.

Jesus came to give his life for people. That was his central goal. He spent a great deal of time challenging and training people. He got them involved in the action. Jesus said to Simon Peter and his brother Andrew:

> Come with me, I will teach you how to bring in people instead of fish. Right then the two brothers dropped their nets and went with him, Matt. 4:19,20, CEV.

The disciples recognized the value, importance and potential of the jobs Jesus was giving them. They would be able to use their abilities and creativity to do their jobs. Jesus trained his people and gave them the opportunity to work for a worthwhile cause. Jesus was constantly training His people so they would be able to spread the Good Word.

Life Cycle of Organizations.

Many managers fail to use their people effectively because the organization's culture and tradition limit the use of creativity. All organizations go through a life cycle similar to people. At birth an organization has not

developed a culture and traditions. In the infancy stage the attitude is, try it and we will see if it will work. There are successes and failures. The successes the managers like and they tend to use them over and over. The things that work become the organization's policies and procedures. The organization begins to develop culture and traditions.

More culture and traditions are added as the organization goes through young adulthood and middle age. This is when the organization moves into its mature phase. In this phase the managers tend to resist innovation and change. Tradition is not inherently bad. Tradition is bad only when it stifles the creativity of the people. The goal of the organization has changed. The new goal is to maintain the traditions of the organization. This hastens the organization's aging process.

In the old age of an organization almost all innovation and creativity ceases. The organization rests on the laurels of its past successes. Its energy is spent on preserving the status quo. New ideas are killed. Some of the comments I am sure you have heard. That will never work. We have never done it that way. Don't rock the boat. Why risk failure when we know what works. At this point the organization begins decaying.

Many organizations die and the only ones who notice it are the people who work there.

Sometimes they do not recognize it. At this stage the organization does not have to die. Every manager should examine the situation and be sure people are being creative. This will be difficult to do at this stage, but if it is not done, the organization will die.

Encourage your people to develop new ways of accomplishing the organization's goals. Every manager must examine his own traditions and insist that his people are encouraged to have new and improved ways of doing their work. If this is done, the organization has an opportunity to recycle and in a sense start over.

Dealing With People's Needs.

A manager will have to deal with a wide variety of peoples needs. To deal with these needs the manager will need some tools to determine what these needs are.

Maslow's Hierarchy of Needs.

Secular managers tend to treat all their people in the same manner. People have different needs. One helpful tool is to classify people according to Maslow's Hierarchy of Needs Theory. Level one will be concerned with his physiological or biological needs. Level two will be concerned with security or safety needs, while level three is concerned with social or belonging needs. Level four is concerned with ego and self esteem needs and level five is concerned with self-fulfillment or self-actualization needs. People will be functioning at work at all these levels, and will have to be dealt with in a different manner .

Watch Test.

Another method of working with people that have different needs is the watch test. Ask a person what time it is. If the person tells you to the minute, he is a watch builder. Watch builders tend to do well at detailed tasks. If a person tells you to the nearest fifteen minutes or half hour, he is a tell-timer. People who are tell timers do well at being told the goal and then turned loose to do the task. They figure out what they need to know and get the job done. A watch builder does not do well at a tell timers job, nor does a tell timer do well at a watch builder's job. The watch test is a very rough way to classify your workers. However it can be quickly done and help you as a manager get work done in a timely manner.

Loyalty Test.

People in an organization roughly can be classified into three groups. The first group is the loyal group. These people are very loyal to the person who is the manager. These people can be thought of as the yes group. When a different person is made manager they will shift their loyalty to that person. Ask their opinion and they will answer with what they think the manager wants to hear. There should be no more than 5% to 10% of these people in an organization.

The second group is the herd. They are called the herd because they will usually go along with what the manager wants. They will follow what the manager wants, so long as it does not interfere with their outside interests too much. On rare occasions they will not do what the manager wants them to do. The herd will generally be 75% to 85% of the people in an organization.

The third group is the why group. You ask these people to do something and they ask why. They tend to be independent thinkers and have to be convinced that what you want them to do will benefit them. You do not want more than 5% to 10% of these people in your organization. If you have more, you will have chaos. Any organization that gets too many of the loyal group or the why group is headed for trouble.

Attitudes.

Our attitudes greatly influence our action. The Bible says,

> You see your face in a mirror and your thoughts in the minds of others, Prov. 27:19, CEV.

This verse shows the powerful influence our thoughts have over our actions. The

Christian manager's attitude has a major role in determining what he does and achieves with people. If a person thinks something is impossible, he usually doesn't bother to try it. In this way our thoughts become a self-fulfilling prophecy.

Negative Thinking

One of the stories about negative thinking comes from Numbers 13, CEV.

Moses sent 12 spies into the Promised Land to determine the size and strength of the cities and the crops raised. Moses did not ask the spies to determine whether it was possible to invade. Their mission was to discover the conditions when they did invade. Upon their return they had a glowing report on its fertility and abundant produce. They reported the people who live there are strong, and the cities are large and walled. The longer they dwelt on the negative the more negative they became.

Ten of the twelve spies said they were too strong for the Israelites. The more they talked and listened to their negative thoughts, the more they thought it was impossible to invade. They said the people were so big, we felt as small as grasshoppers.

Negative thinking always produces negative conclusions. Later we read in the book of Joshua that the assumptions they made were false.

The spies' negative report spread like wildfire among the people of Israel. They cried all night saying, if only we had died in Egypt, or in the desert! Is the Lord leading us into Canaan, just to have us killed and our women and children captured?

Negative attitudes are highly contagious. The negative thinking of the ten spies infected the entire nation. For the next 40 years that generation of negative thinkers wandered through the wilderness until all the negative thinkers died. They did not take the Promised Land because they did not think they could.

After 40 years of wandering, their children had replaced the negative thinkers. Joshua was now the leader of Israel.

The people of Israel came to the banks of the Jordan River and they saw the promised land that God had wanted to give to their parent's years before. Again spies were sent to Jericho. They spent the night with a prostitute named Rahab. She recognized the men as spies, Israelites, by the clothes they wore. She told them the people had been terrified of them because of the way their God fought for them. See Js. 2, CEV.

Keep in mind the people of Jericho, who were so afraid of Israel, were the children of those who a generation before had first heard of Israel and their great God.

The spies returned to Joshua and the people of Israel and said they were sure the Lord has given us this country. The people shake with fear every time they think of us. See Js. 2: 24, CEV.

This time the spies gave a positive report. The Israelites were motivated to take positive action and within days they had taken Jericho. What was the difference between the two generations? It was a positive attitude rather than a negative attitude. Christian managers must keep in mind that the power of negative thinking is just as great as the power of positive thinking. Negative thinking is one of Satan's most powerful tools.

The Power of Positive Thinking.

The power of positive thinking promotes the idea that by thinking positively, a person can turn desire into reality. Our attitudes greatly influences our actions, but we must not be deceived by thinking that our mental power alone is sufficient to accomplish our plans. This is the philosophy of many of those who promote the power of positive thinking without God being involved. God makes it clear that left to ourselves, we have little power over many of our circumstances. This is what the Lord says:

> *I, the Lord, have put a curse on those who turn from me and trust in human strength. They will dry up like a bush in salty desert sand where nothing grows. But I will bless those who trust in me, Jer.* 17: 5, 7. CEV.

This passage shows the falsehood of trusting solely in people and only in human resourcefulness to solve problems. What a contrast between the person who trusts himself and the person who trusts God. The power of positive thinking without God focuses on human resources while the power of positive thinking with God focuses on God as the resource. How much of God's power is available to the Christian manager?

> *I pray that Jesus Christ and the church forever bring praise to God. His power at work in us can do far more than we dare to ask or imagine Amen,* Eph. 3: 20, CEV.

Show me a person with small goals and I will show you a person with a small God. The size of our God reflects the size of our goals.

Everything you ask for in prayer will be yours, if you only have faith, Mark 11:24, CEV.

God can produce more than we are capable of asking for. We must do the asking and what we say God may grant.

Many managers allow their attitudes to be controlled by past circumstances. Look to the future, not the past. Look to the future with anticipation. Always have a goal. View problems as an opportunity for improvement. In James it is written:

My friends be glad even if you have a lot of trouble, James 1: 2, CEV.

Why should you be happy when facing problems? James then said:

You know that you learn to endure by having your faith tested, James 1: 3,CEV.

The manager's attitudes have a major role in the outcome of a group's work. Attitudes are very contagious. One individual's negative attitude can affect the group. The successful manager must always know the attitudes and morale within his group. One does not have positive attitudes simply by telling himself to think positively. To maintain a positive outlook, focus on God and his resources.

The attitudes that you carry are often difficult for you to recognize. With a trusted friend, ask them to tell you what attitudes are coming across. This should not be done by a person who works for you, but someone that knows you well in the work setting.

Motivation.

The early church was built by leaders appointed by Christ. There is no question they were highly motivated. These leaders were convinced that what they had to do was essential to the people. They passed this conviction on to their followers. Motivation comes from within an individual. The only thing that managers can do is provide an environment that will stimulate employees to be motivated.

Many managers believe money is the motivator that works best. Research has found that money does motivate, but only for a short while. Other things, such as the organizations mission and goals, do not motivate many employees, even if they know what the mission and goals are.

Motivation and job satisfaction run in cycles. Sometimes they will be high but often they will be low. Employees typically do not see that their efforts are making a difference to management or to the organization, much less to society. At times the employee's feeling of lack of contribution can end up as employee burnout or a mid-life crises.

A Christian manager has to realize his employees have different needs that will help them to motivate themselves. Use of the Maslow's hierarchy of needs is a good place to start to find what will motivate different groups of employees. Keep in mind that motivation comes from within an individual. You, as manager, can help create the environment that will help with an employees motivation.

Behavior Modification

What goes hand in hand with motivation is behavior modification. A foundation of being a Christian is when you recognizes your past life style may no longer be serving you well. If so a fundamental change is both necessary but more importantly desired.

Christ first modeled the desired change and then provided support. It has been passed on to us with His written word. His model was a lifestyle based upon servant leadership. Intrinsic with this lifestyle is a relationship with Jesus. Ingrained in this relationship is a lifestyle that is based upon ethics and morality. Much of these standard ethics comes from the Old Testament. This foundation of change based on common ethics serving mankind applies to every aspect of life, including your conduct in your work environment.

There have been many books written on how to change the way an employee thinks in order to make him a team player for the organization. These books almost always center on some type of short-term action that will bring about a positive reaction on the part of the employee. Usually this becomes a cause and effect process, often without the employees knowledge.

The employee rarely becomes dedicated to the mission of the organization. The employee usually returns to his previous attitude and comfort level. No long term motivation takes place because the employee does not change his foundational beliefs.

Chapter Six

TEAMWORK
DELEGATION

Team Defined.

A team can be defined as two or more people working together toward a common goal. Key words are two or more people, working together and common goal. Unless these three elements are present, a team does not exist. If two or more people are not communicating, there is no team. The purpose of a team is to help people accomplish more than they could individually. See Ecc. 4:9-13, CEV. Both quality and quantity of production will improve if there is an effective team.

Jesus knew and used this principle of an effective team consistently. He formed a team of twelve men and trained them to carry on with His work after he left them.

Jesus divided His men into two man teams and sent them out to preach the gospel, heal the sick and cast out demons, See Mark 6: 7-13, CEV.

Why did Jesus not send out twelve individuals? Because he understood team dynamics. If people learn to work together as a team, they will be more effective than if they work alone. Jesus taught His disciples to work together as a team to accomplish a common goal.

Strengths and Weaknesses.

A team allows people to use their gifts, skills, and talents more effectively. Everyone has strengths and weaknesses. One's weaknesses tend to reduce the effectiveness of his strengths. One purpose of a team is to bring people together to compensate for each other's weaknesses. A team can be any number of people. The disciples were a team as well as the two man teams Christ sent out to preach the Good Word.

Christ chose some of us to be apostles, prophets, missionaries, pastors and teachers, so that his people would learn to serve and his body grow strong, Eph. 4: 11,12, CEV.

God does not expect an individual to be strong in every area. Each person has been given his own unique set of gifts, skills, creative talents and weaknesses. Many managers think that one of their duties is to eliminate or at least reduce people's weaknesses. When people are teamed together they balance their strengths and their weaknesses. This approach to team building gives people more job satisfaction, more motivation and greater productivity. People are always happier and more productive when they can work at something they are good at and enjoy. However, this does not mean that people should ignore their shortcomings and turn down opportunities to develop new skills.

Team Members Needs.

Members of a team bring needs to that team. There are four needs that all team members bring to the team. One is the need to use one's skills and gifts to assist the team's efforts. Another is the need to be accepted by other team members. The need to pursue team goals compatible with personal goals, as well as the need to represent people and groups outside the team are some of the needs. The team goal or mission is key to developing and maintaining a productive team. A manager should involve the team members in developing or refining the team goal thus giving the team ownership of the team goal.

Team Dynamics.

Team dynamics play an important part in a team's successes or failures. Each individual is continually playing a positive or negative role within the team. Positive roles are production and maintenance roles. The negative roles can best be defined as anti-team roles.

- Production roles focus on a task or job. Members contributing to team production generally play one or more of the following roles.

- Organizer: works with the group to identify, assign and schedule tasks.

- Initiator: offers for the group's consideration proposals and recommendations that can be discussed.

- Data Collector: gathers facts, figures and other information needed to assist the group.

- Facilitator: helps maintain a constant flow of information needed in order for the team to achieve the goal.

- Evaluator: studies results and assists in making adjustments when needed.

- Maintenance rolls focus on assisting others on the team. Every individual as needed should assume the following roles.

- Encourager: works at building positive morale among the team and promotes ideas and actions of others.

- Follower: allows others to take the lead and use their abilities whenever possible.

- Negotiator: attempts to mediate conflict and be willing to compromise on issues and personal views for the benefit of the team.

- Protector: tries to shield fellow team member's from outside distractions.

- Servant: does whatever he can to meet the needs of each team member.

- Anti-team roles focus on self. Each team member should avoid assuming any of these roles because they hamper team production.

- Dominator: tries to control conversation, ideas and actions within the team.

- Blocker: delays, sidetracks or stops progress.

- Attention Seeker: tries to get the team to focus on him continually and recognize him for his accomplishments, real or imagined.

- Avoider: refuses to deal with issues, facts and personal obligations.

When forming the team the manager should explain all the roles and encourage the group to watch for anti-team roles. Each team member should be committed to avoiding anti-team roles. When these anti-team roles appear, and they will appear, fellow team members should confront the guilty team member and help him to return to production and maintenance roles.

Delegation.

Delegation is the transferring of authority, responsibility and accountability from one person or group to another. This is usually moving authority from a higher level to a lower level in an organization. Delegation is one of the techniques to decentralize an organization. It allows more people to become involved in the decision-making process. Exodus 18: 13-26, (CEV) is all about delegation. Moses resembled present-day managers. He was providing strong spiritual leadership, but he lacked the management skills needed to do the job God had called him to do. This passage in Exodus describes a typical day in Moses' life.

People were waiting to get a decision by Moses. This taking of Moses' time must have greatly reduced their progress as they traveled. Moses' father-in-law, Jethro asked Moses why he was the only judge, and the people had to wait on him all day?

Jethro asked probing questions. In answering Moses spoke of his philosophy of leadership and management. He said as the spiritual leader he was in a better position to act as judge. Jethro told Moses that what he was doing was not as good as it should be. You and these people who come to you will only wear yourselves out. The work is too heavy for you and you should not handle it alone.

Jethro explained to Moses that he should divide the decision-making power and delegate it to trustworthy men. That will make your workload lighter because they will share it with you. . Moses admitted he had a problem and was willing to change, even if it meant giving some of his authority for decisions to others.

Many modern managers will not delegate because they feel they do not have competent, trustworthy and experienced people to delegate too. The people Moses picked served as judges for the people. The difficult cases they brought to Moses but the simple cases they decided themselves. The people that Moses delegated to had no experience in serving as judges. The word trustworthy does not mean Moses picked people who had experience. Trustworthy means he picked men who were honest and could be trusted.

Delegation makes the manager's job easier. It increases productivity and it develops additional leadership. Delegation gives the Christian manager more time for his personal spiritual development. Delegation also stimulates employee creativity and demonstrates trust and confidence in employee ability. It stimulates employee motivation and commitment to the organization. Most managers need to delegate more.

I have never met a manager who is delegating everything he should. Managers who have not delegated enough are easily spotted in an organization. They often skip coffee breaks and lunch time to work. They frequently come in on weekends to catch up on the work.

Delegation Methods.

Recognize the limits of your capacity to do your work. Most managers do not do this until they can no longer do all the work. Know the purpose of your delegation. It may be just to give the manager more time or perhaps to train others to be managers.

Knowing the purpose of delegation will influence greatly what is delegated and to whom. Select the jobs or projects or parts of projects to be delegated. Select the person or persons for delegation. It should not be the first one that comes to mind but one that will make sure the project will be done. Jethro told Moses,

> *You will need to appoint some competent leaders who respect God and are trustworthy and*

honest. Then put them over groups of ten, fifty, a hundred and a thousand, Exodus 18: 21, CEV.

Select the person or persons to be given the assignment. When doing this, there are several questions to ask yourself. Which employee is best suited for the job in terms of experience and training? What is the interest in the job by the employee being considered? Will the person selected have the time to do the delegated work and be able to do his regular job as well? When can the employee begin? Will the employee need special assistance or training to do the delegated job? Meet with the person selected for the delegated job and explain all instructions, requirements and other important factors that are being delegated.

- Make sure the person understands the following about the job.
- When the assignment begins.
- All instructions on how the project must be done.
- The decision-making power he will have.
- What resources he will have.
- Special procedures involved in the work.
- Whom the employee will go to when he needs help.

- The purpose of the work.

- The importance of the work.

- Where it fits with other projects and activities.

- How the employee will be evaluated.

Not understanding any of these points can lead to problems, even failure. Take as much time as necessary to be sure the employee understands. Have communications with the employee while he works on the job. Keeping open communications with the employee helps to avoid unforeseen problems. The employee will know that you are interested and available to help with the project. Keep informed about the project but do not interfere with the person you have delegated the project too. Be lavish with praise.

Elements of Delegation.

The most important elements of delegation are responsibility, authority and accountability.

Responsibility pertains to the activity to be performed. Make sure the employee knows what is to be done.

Authority concerns the decision-making power needed to perform the assigned work.

Accountability is the obligation to perform duties in a responsible manner and exercise the authority given in terms of the performance standards.

Never assign responsibility without giving the authority needed to do the job. Many managers are reluctant to delegate because it might cause them to lose control of the results.

Failure to specify the boundary lines of authority creates many of the problems in delegation. Boundary lines of authority allow the manager to anticipate the decisions and actions of his subordinates. Boundaries protect both the worker and the manager by identifying where decision-making power ends and recommendations begin. Authority boundaries help eliminate confusion as to who is responsible for making decisions on any activity. This ties into accountability for actions and results.

God set the example for delegation. Psalm 8 describes God's philosophy and attitude toward delegation.

> *I often think of the heavens Your hands have made and of the moon and stars You put into place. Then I ask. Why do You care about us humans? Why are You concerned for us weaklings? You made us a little lower than Yourself and You have crowned us with glory and honor. You let us rule everything Your hands have made, and You*

put it all under our power, *Ps. 8: 3-6, CEV.*

What a display of trust, confidence and love. If God is willing to put us in charge of what He had so perfectly made, why shouldn't the Christian manager be willing to delegate authority, responsibility and accountability to those who work for him.

This granting of delegation should be a well thought out process. It should not be something that just happens. Sooner or later there will be a dispute between the manager and the person that has assumed delegation. This is a position that all concerned do not want to get into.

Too often people get on the job and are given little or no training for the work they are expected to do. They are then faced with a sink or swim situation. Adequate training of supervisors and all team members is an absolute requirement if the team is to produce in an exemplary manner. Training all too often is not done until you realize your project is in trouble. If this is the situation and you can, stop the project and do the training.

Chapter Seven

Decision-Making
Problem Solving

Knowing God's Will.

How does one go about making the right decisions?

You will show the right path to all who worship you, Ps 25: 12, CEV.

How will He teach us to choose the best decision? Knowing God's will is the foundation for decision making. The Christian manager has a unique ability in his decision-making process. It is based on knowing that God does have a specific plan for us and that plan can be known. To know that plan you must understand how to know God's will. Many Christian managers are confused about God's will for them and their organization. Many feel they cannot figure out what God wants them to do.

The process of knowing God's will is not too complicated. The Bible gives us a simple process. Too often we do not spend enough time studying God's word. Many of us are not listening to God and therefore don't understand what He says. Too many of us think God has to use spectacular means for us to hear him, such as Moses and the parting of the Red Sea.

Jesus made that clear when talking to the scribes and Pharisees who were seeking a special sign. See Matt. 12: 38-39, CEV.

Elijah learned that God does not need special means to communicate his will.

> All at once strong wind shook the mountain and shattered the rocks. But the Lord was not in the wind. Next there was an earthquake. But the Lord was not in the earthquake. Then there was a fire. But the Lord was not in the fire.
>
> Finally there was a gentle breeze and when Elijah heard it, he covered his face with his coat. He went out and stood at the entrance to the cave. The Lord asked Elijah why are you here?1 Kings 19: 11-13, CEV.

Elijah learned the Lord can speak in a soft whisper, not necessarily with spectacular events.

One must be committed to learning God's will in order to know your will. God does not waste his time revealing his will to people who do not want to listen. One might say that we have free will, so how can God have a plan for us? We do have free will, but God knows what we will plan before we do. If it is pleasing to

God, then we will know because it will be pleasing to us in our heart. Paul said:

> *Dear friends, God is good. I beg you to offer your bodies to Him . I beg you to offer your bodies to Him as a living sacrifice, pure and pleasing.* That's the *most sensible way to serve God. Don't be like the people of this world, but let God change the way you think. Then you will know how to do everything that is good and pleasing to him,* Ro 12: 11-13,CEV.

In this passage Paul states that we will find God's will only after we have committed ourselves to Him. He also tells us that God's will for us is good and pleasing and, in fact, perfect. Paul was able to make the right decisions because he had met the prerequisite for knowing the good and pleasing and perfect will of God. Paul became totally committed to doing the will of God.

God Has A Plan.

Recognize that God has a plan. Throughout the Bible God makes it clear He has a plan for His people.

> *I will bless you with a future filled with hope—a future of success, not of suffering,* Jer. 29: 11, CEV.

You said to me, I will point out the road that you should follow. I will be your teacher and watch over you, Ps. 32: 8,CEV.

How does he tell us what he wants done? God tells us His will by giving us a desire to do what he wants done.

God is working in you to make you willing and able to obey Him, Phil. 2: 13, CEV.

Your Desire.

God's promises are in Psalm 37, and Philippians 2.

Do what the Lord wants, and he will give you your heart's desire, Ps. 37: 4, CEV.

God is working in you to make you willing and able to obey him. Phil. 2: 13, CEV.

Some people say your desires could be coming from Satan. The scriptures do not say God will give you every desire of your heart. God's promise is conditional. If we meet the requirement of being totally committed to God and his will for us, then God will give us the desires of our heart..

According to Philippians 2: 13, God put the desire in our heart. If the desire is from God, He will provide the means, the power and resources to be sure the desire can be accomplished. However, it is possible to have the desire and the resources and still not be according to God's will.

> *The Lord gives perfect peace to those whose faith is firm,* Isa 26: 3, CEV..

God promises us peace as long as we operate within His will. If we have the desire and the resources, but do not have peace, we should question what we want.

Four Key Questions.

There are four key questions to determine God's will in a decision-making situation.

- Am I committed to doing God's will? See Rom. 12; 13, CEV.

- Is it the desire of my heart to pursue this decision? See Ps. 37: 4,CEV.

- Does God provide the power and means to accomplish this decision? See Phil 2: 13, CEV.

- Does God give me peace to make the decisions necessary for my endeavor? See Isa. 26: 3, CEV.

Unless one can say yes to all four questions, one should think long and hard about not pursuing a project.

Five Steps For Decision Making.

The Bible has a five-step process for decision-making. These are the same five steps found in many management texts. The difference for the Christian manager is the Biblical foundations for each step. These five steps are a means to logically reach the best decision.

Diagnose The Issue.

Step One is to correctly diagnose the issue or problem. If the diagnosis is not correctly made it will be wrong and it could be costly to correct it. The story of Moses sending out 12 men to gain information about Canaan is an example. See Num. 13: 1-2, CEV. The men incorrectly diagnosed the situation and as a result, the people of Israel spent 40 years wandering in the desert.

Gather Facts.

Step Two is to gather and analyze the facts. Gathering and analyzing data is important in the decision-making process.

It's stupid and embarrassing to give an answer before you listen, Prov. 18: 13, CEV.

Know the facts. There is great value in what the Bible says on decision-making.

*Never stop reading the Book of
the Law he gave you,* Josh. 1: 8,
CEV.

*Ask Me, and I will tell you things
you don't know and can't find out,*
Jer. 33: 3, CEV.

Are you committed to doing the will of
God? See Rom 12: 1-2, CEV, discussed
earlier. What are my interests and desires?

*Do what the Lord wants and He
will give you your heart's desire,* Ps.
37: 4, CEV.

Gathering facts and data has to be done
with care. However you must realize that you
cannot get all the data. Get as much data as
you can and move on. When you feel you have
the essential data it is time to proceed to step
three.

Develop Alternatives.

Step Three is to develop alternatives.
Important decisions should never be made until
alternatives have been developed. The first
choice one makes may not be the best one.
Developing alternatives forces one to look
more closely at the data and to think through all
the choices. It also helps one not to solve
problems too quickly. One of the alternatives
should be to do nothing at all. Look at this
alternative and what will happen if you do
nothing at all.

Evaluate The Alternatives.

Step Four is to Evaluate the Alternatives. Each one of the alternatives should be evaluated for its strengths and weaknesses. This step will eliminate some of the alternatives. Jesus taught an example of this step.

> *What will a king do if he has only ten thousand soldiers to defend himself against a king who is about to attack him with twenty thousand soldiers? Before he goes to battle, won't he sit down and decide if he can win? If he thinks he won't be able to defend himself, he will send messengers and ask for peace while the other king is a long way off,* Lk. 14: 31-33, CEV.

This passage points out evaluations in terms of positive and negative impact. A negative alternative means a no decision, while a positive alternative means a possible decision.

Select Best Alternative.

Step Five: Select the best of the positive alternatives. This step is usually the most difficult. Many managers hesitate on decision-making because they are not sure they will make the best choice. The Christian manager should keep in mind God's promise.

You said to me. I will point out the road that you should follow. I will be your teacher and watch over you, Ps. 32:8, CEV.

This step will be easier if you have the assistance and advice by working with those who gathered the data.

The Organizational Climate.

The decision-making process always happens in a certain climate. Every Christian manager must be aware of the nature of this climate in his organization.

What is the need for action? The manager should always ask himself the question. Is there need for this action? In a situation that needs a decision conditions degenerate as the need for action is delayed. As conditions degenerate, the manager is put under more pressure for a decision. As time goes on, the possibility of making a right decision decreases. A decision should be made as close as possible to the time it is needed.

Is there sufficient data. With every decision, it is true that more data, facts and information could have been gathered and used. However, one never has the luxury of having all the facts to make a decision. There comes a time when the decision must be made regardless of how much data one has. The insufficient data trap can lead to stalling, which causes degenerating conditions and poor decisions.

Each decision contains an element of risk. A good manager learns to calculate risks and make them work for him in the decision-making process. The wise manager knows he cannot eliminate all risk. Risks usually decrease as facts and information increase.

The greater the possibility of failure, the stronger the feeling of risk. This fear of failure is very detrimental to the decision process. The manager cannot allow himself to dwell on the risk of failure. Accept the fact that failure is always possible and move on with the decision-making process.

Every manager knows his success depends upon his ability to make good decisions. In contrast to the results of failure, the rewards of success are great for making the right decision at the right time.

There is the existence of more than one workable solution. Many managers struggle with the idea that they must make the one best decision. A poor decision properly implemented frequently works better that a good decision improperly implemented. Therefore a manager must give as much thought to the implementing as the decision.

Decision Making; Problem Solving

Problem solving involves making decisions, but not all decisions are involved in problem solving. Decision-making can be defined as choosing between alternatives. Problem solving is the process of formulating and implementing a plan of action to solve a problem.

In this process there may be many decisions that have to be made. Simply making a decision may not solve the problem. This is something you will find out through experience. You will find yourself being more comfortable with making decisions as you grow in your job. Keep in mind that a wrong decision may be much better than no decision at all.

Problems and Conditions

It is important to understand the difference between problems and conditions. A condition is a uncontrollable circumstance from outside the problem. Conditions usually require a considerable length of time to change.

If a manager assumes conditions are problems, he will become frustrated, be confused and have low morale. He will become discouraged because he fails to get results. The manager should identify the problems created by outside conditions and attempt to solve these problems over time.

Problem solving requires a method of eliminating a difficulty. A process of problem solving can be done by with the following steps.

- First, determine if the situation is a condition or a problem.

- Second, if a problem exists clearly state the problem. The manager should get as much input as possible to identify the problem correctly.

- If the manager gets emotionally involved in solving the problem, emotions tend to distort reality. The more involved the manager becomes the greater the need for outside assistance in determining the real problem.

- Third, determine what will be gained or lost in solving the problem. Make sure solving this problem does not create a bigger problem.

- Fourth, identify alternate methods and solutions. This is a critical step and requires as much input as possible. It helps if the persons who will be involved in carrying out the solution are involved in the selection of the alternative to be implemented.

A city without wise leaders will end up in ruin. A city with many wise leaders will be kept safe, Prov. 11: 14, CEV.

- Fifth. Determine the cost of each alternative. The cost may not be just in dollars, but in time, energy, attitudes and public opinion. This cost factor plays a big role in determining what alternative will be selected. To select an alternative which may be the best one but has costs you cannot afford is asking for failure that may extend beyond the project itself.

- Sixth: Select the alternative. Consider the following when making a selection of what to implement. Does this solution violate biblical truth or principle? Does this solution meet the needs of the people affected? Will people support implementing the solution? Will this solution create other problems? Why should this alternative be selected over other alternatives?

- Seventh: Delegate action and begin implementation. The problem will not be eliminated just by making a decision, but by implementing actions that will bring about the change wanted.

- Eighth: Evaluate progress. Each action step should be watched and evaluated to determine if the action is helping the solution of the problem. If not, corrective action or new alternatives may have to be developed and implemented until the problem is solved. This step is often not done until the project is so out of control it is difficult to correct it. It is important that this step is done in a timely manner.

The Christian Managers Job.

The Christian manager's job is to serve the work related needs of those who work for him.

They served as judges, deciding the easy cases themselves, but bringing the difficult ones to Moses, Ex. 18: 26, CEV.

The effective Christian manager gives himself to help those who work for him with problems they cannot solve alone, but letting them solve the problems they can. Problems which they cannot solve alone the relationship of the manager and employee must be open.

The employee must feel comfortable with bringing the problem to his manager. The employee must also be open and comfortable in going to his peers for help.. Through experience the employee will learn when he has reached a point where he cannot solve a problem alone.

Chapter Eight

Communication

What is Communication?

Communication can be defined as the process we go through to convey understanding from one person or group to another. We have developed sophisticated electronic devices to communicate. Yet many people have difficulty with face-to-face communication. Many management texts have communication as the number one difficulty of managers.

The difficulty we have in communication is that you want the receiver of a message to understand it the same way as it was sent. Unfortunately, the receiver understands it the way he thinks he heard it. Jesus knew the importance of communication. Jesus worked hard to make sure understanding occurred between Him and the disciples. After sharing some parables with the disciples Jesus wanted to make sure they had understood.

Jesus asked his disciples if they understood all these things? They answered, Yes, we do, Matt. 13: 51, CEV.

Jesus understood very well that there was no communication unless understanding occurred, regardless of how much preaching or lecturing He did.

Tower of Babel.

. The tower of Babel story is about communication. At that time there was only one language spoken by everyone.. God told of the importance of communication by saying.

> *Come on! Let's go down and confuse them by making them speak different languages—then they won't be able to understand each other,* Gen. 11: 7, CEV.

Once their being able to understand each other communications were disrupted, the building of the tower came to a standstill. This story of the tower of Babel illustrates the important role communication plays in any organization. If it breaks down, a project will probably fail.

Communication Steps.

God and science confirms that communication plays one of the most vital roles in any organization's success. There are six steps to the communication process. The first three must be taken by the person transmitting the message and the last three by the person receiving the message.

- Step One: The transmitter must develop a clear concept of the idea or feeling to be communicated. If one does not have a clear understanding of what he wants to say, those hearing him will not have a clear understanding of what he is saying.

- Step Two: Choose the right words and actions to convey the idea or feeling. Ideas and feelings must be conveyed or there will not be understanding by the receivers. We must understand that withholding ideas and feelings is one of the greatest causes of misunderstanding.

- Step Three: Become aware of surrounding communication barriers and work at minimizing them. Communication represents the lifeblood of an organization. If there are barriers and the communication is not understood by part of an organization, that part will become ineffective. It is important to identify barriers to communication. Most of them can be minimized.

A communication barrier can be anything that inhibits or distorts efforts to communicate. Note that it is impossible to eliminate all barriers to communication. One of these barriers is tuning people out and hearing only what one wants to hear. Another barrier is to allow personal emotion to distort the information. One emotion is a lack of trust in other people's motives. Other barriers are noise or other distractions as well as differing value systems and perceptions.

A frequent barrier is unwillingness to receive information that conflicts with preconceived notions or viewpoints. Words that have several different meanings can also be a barrier. The sender's actions not corresponding with what he is saying is also a barrier to communications.

- Step Four: The receiver must absorb the transmitted information by listening to the words and observing the actions. In this way the listener plays a very important role in the communications process. A great deal of the senders original meaning can be lost in this step.

- Step Five: The listener must translate the words and actions of the speaker. This translation of words and actions of the speaker is very critical to understanding what he is saying.. A great deal of the original meaning can be lost during this step in the communication process.

- Step Six: The receiver must develop correct ideas and/or feelings based upon the message from the sender. If the idea that was sent in step one is the same idea received in step six, understanding has occurred. If the idea being sent is not the idea received, misunderstanding exists and communication has broken down.

Communication barriers can be minimized and greatly reduced by applying the following techniques.

- Whenever possible use face to face communications.

- Use direct and simple words.

- Solicit feedback from the listener.

- Give full attention to the speaker.

- Never interrupt the speaker because he is not ready to listen until he finishes speaking.

- Encourage freedom of expression.

- Agree to disagree.

- Be willing to accept the other person's ideas and feelings whether in agreement with them or not.

These techniques seem very simple to do, however in actual practice they can be difficult. If you have to opportunity to take a listening course it is recommended. Often you will in the heat of the moment not remember or follow the techniques above. When this happens it is usually best to halt the conversation if you have that option.

Listening.

Listening plays an important role in the communication process. Studies reveal that the average person spends approximately seventy percent of his waking day in verbal communication, forty-five percent of which is spent listening. Further research indicates that unless people have had specific training in listening, their efficiency in this skill is about twenty-five percent. In America we generally are not a listening culture.

We are particularly deficient in the skill of listening, especially when we are communicating with another person one on one. There are cultures in the world that are listening cultures.

The difficulty in listening is caused by the fact that the average person can listen at a rate of 400 to 600 words a minute. Most people speak at only 200 to 400 words a minute. As a result, in conversation the mind tends to occupy itself with other things about half of the time. This wandering of the mind causes the listener to miss a great deal of the ideas and feelings being presented.

Another facet of our communication culture in America is that we cannot tolerate silence. The average American will begin speaking if there is 10 to 15 seconds of silence in a conversation. As an experiment, when talking to someone, stop conversing. See how quick the other person starts to speak.

There are some things that can done to improve listening skills.

Do not be afraid to ask questions to help you understand. Failure to ask questions is the most common listener weakness and creates failure to understand what the speaker meant.

Do not start formulating your response while the speaker is still talking. We do not wait because we would rather talk than listen.

Avoid second guessing what the speaker is going to say. When you speak the words to finish the speakers sentence is very annoying to the speaker. This action on your part may make a conversation that is amiable change to almost hostile.

There is a time for listening and a time for speaking, Ecc. 3: 7, CEV.

Some of the things that can happen when you interrupt are listed below.

The complete message of the sender is disrupted, making it more difficult to understand what was intended. The speaker has difficulty listening because his mind is on what he is saying.

By interrupting the listener has demonstrated what he has to say is more important than what the speaker has to say.

By interrupting the listener has made an assumption about what the speaker was going to say, which may be in error.

Work on minimizing the effect of prejudices that filter and distort your understanding. If you have an awareness of your prejudices, ask clarifying questions to help you understand. This is difficult to do for many people since they often do not know their prejudices, or if they do they do not call them with that label.

Listen for the ideas and feelings being spoken. Some studies report that in certain situations, only 7% of the message is communicated by the words spoken. The remaining 93% is transmitted through voice tone or other nonverbal action or expression, such as body language. We must learn to hear more than the words being spoken. We must become active listeners. Paul talked of this listening ability when he said,

People of Athens, I see you are religious, Acts 17: 22, CEV.

Paul observed their actions as well as their words. He did more than just listen to the people of Athens. You need to do this whenever possible. Even when you are talking on the telephone listen to more than just the words. The subtle change in voice tones can help you understand the caller better.

Active Listening.

Mark 8: 13-21. CEV gives us a classic example of Jesus' disciples failing to use active listening and as a result misunderstanding what Jesus was saying.

After the feeding of the 4000, Jesus and his disciples got in a boat and headed across the Sea of Galilee. During the trip Jesus told the disciples to avoid the leaven of the Pharisees. The disciples discussed this among themselves and decided he was reprimanding them for failing to bring bread. Overhearing them talk, Jesus commanded them.

Why are you talking about having no bread? Don't you understand? Are your minds still closed? Are your eyes blind and your ears deaf?
Mark 8: 17-18, CEV.

The disciples had been poor listeners for several reasons. They were listening only to the words Jesus spoke and not to the ideas and feelings behind the words. They were not active listeners. They failed to ask clarifying questions and discussed only among themselves. As a result they totally misunderstood the point of Jesus' admonition.

Jesus was not concerned about a lack of bread having just fed the 4000 with seven loaves. Jesus was speaking about the sin and lack of faith of the Pharisees as evidenced by his conversation with them prior to leaving in the boat. See Mark 8:11-12, CEV. This passage is an example of poor listening by only listening to Jesus words. It is also an example of how people are reluctant to ask clarifying questions. Jesus was an excellent communicator and saw they did not understand what he was saying. Therefore he clarified his statement.

Certain attitudes are needed for active listening. The listener must develop an attitude of wanting to hear the speaker. Eye contact is one of the best ways of letting the speaker know that you want to hear what he is saying. Using eye contact helps with nonverbal communications. The listener must be willing to accept the ideas and feelings of the speaker. This does not necessarily mean you agree with the speaker. One must be willing to let the speaker have his own views, opinions, ideas and feelings. Keep in mind that the feelings of a person represent his real self.

Attitudes of wanting to hear the speaker are very important when dealing with controversial issues that could lead to conflict. Your recognizing the speakers right to his views helps you to avoid becoming defensive.

It is stupid to say bad things about your neighbors. If you are sensible you you will keep quiet, Prov. 11:12, CEV.

When speaking you must focus on keeping your words simple. Paul wrote to the Corinthians.

Friends, when I came and told you the mystery that God has shared with us, I didn't use big words or try to sound wise, 1 Cor. 2:1, CEV.

Paul was a great communicator because of his ability to present great truths in simple easy to understand language. This is important if you are to become an excellent communicator.

Unfortunately the trend today is to use nondescript, multi-syllable words that carry very little meaning for most people. Some of the greatest statements made were the simplest. The Lord's prayer contains 56 words. The Gettysburg Address only 267 words. The Declaration of Independence has 1,322 words. In contrast a recent government publication on the sale of grain contains 26,901 words. The trend to wordiness is a major cause of our communication problems today.

Body Language.

Non-verbal communication is made up in great part by body language. The active listener must make a conscious effort to learn the speaker's body language. The listener must be aware of what the speaker is communicating. A number of books tell what the mainstream American body language means.

For example, the arms crossed and folded usually means, I don't believe you. The arms open and extended a little means, I am receptive to what you want to say. We all are aware of body language, often subconsciously. It improves communication if you become aware of body language and you becomes good at interpreting body language. Learn to become an active listener including body language.

Chapter Nine

Conflict

Conflict Defined

On occasion managers will find themselves involved directly or indirectly in a conflict within their organization or with another organization. Conflict is a potentially dangerous capable of destroying the effectiveness of any organization or manager.

The Bible describes the potential of conflict.

> But if you keep attacking each other like wild animals, you had better watch out or you will destroy yourselves, Gal. 5: 15, CEV.

Conflict can be defined as open and hostile opposition occurring as a result of differing viewpoints. This is not to be confused with disagreement. It is possible to have disagreements without hostility Conflict always involves hostility. No part of an organization is immune from conflict either between individuals or among groups within the organization.

Conflict comes from our selfish desires and passions. See James 4: 1, CEV. The emphasis is on self. We focus on me and mine, my ideas, my rights and my feelings. In Proverbs we read,

> *Too much pride causes trouble.*
> *Be sensible and take advice,*
> Prov13: 10, CEV.

When in conflict, our conversation is saturated with statements that promote, protect and draw attention to ourselves. The purpose of conflict is almost always to impose our ideas, beliefs, desires and opinions on others.

Conflict causes us to fabricate and magnify faults and weaknesses in others. We are convinced our position is correct and the other person's must be wrong. It is almost impossible to limit negative feelings and thoughts toward others when in conflict. When the issues of conflict are not kept in focus, we attack the person. Conflict creates division within an organization. Jesus said,

> *Any kingdom where people fight*
> *each other will end up ruined. A*
> *town or family that fights will*
> *destroy itself,* Matt. 12: 25, CEV.

Conflict causes us to expend our energies on nonproductive activities. Conflict leaves people physically and emotionally drained.

Methods of Dealing With Conflict.

Attempt to avoid conflict by retreating from it.

There are many ways to do this. The most popular one is to procrastinate. The conflict can never by solved by retreating from it. The longer we avoid the conflict usually the worse it becomes. The scriptures tell us,

> Don't get so angry that you sin. Don't go to bed angry and don't give the devil a chance, Eph. 4: 26-27, CEV.

Attempt to avoid conflict by going around the major issues and focus on minor issues.

As long as we focus on minor issues there is little chance of resolution. We must be willing to honestly work with the real issues involved.

Attempt to avoid the conflict by dealing with side issues.

This is probably the most dangerous method of trying to deal with conflict. You are trying to deal with side issues in an attempt to divert attention away from the real conflict. This frequently leads to more conflict.

There will be misunderstanding and confusion if the person continues to resist resolving the conflict. If this occurs then you may need to dissolve the relationship. Once you have done everything you can to resolve the problem and the other person refuses to cooperate, the relationship should be terminated. See Matt. 18: 17, CEV.

In the event the other person is willing to repent and correct the problem, you are obligated to forgive and continue the relationship.

Correct any followers of mine who sin and forgive the ones who say they are sorry. Even if one mistreats you seven times in one day and says, I am sorry, you should forgive that person, Luke 17: 3-4, CEV.

It makes you look good when you avoid a fight, only fools love to quarrel, Prov. 20: 3, CEV.

Conflict should be avoided. If it happens you should deal with it honestly and quickly and if possible in private.

Disagreement..

Disagreement versus conflict. Conflict always involves hostility, but you can have disagreement without hostility or ill will. In some cases disagreement can be beneficial Disagreement can lead to growth. A positive change can happen with a disagreement.

As iron sharpens iron, friends sharpen the minds of each other, Prov. 27: 17, CEV.

Disagreements can reveal the need for change. A manager should welcome healthy disagreement because it forces him to evaluate the situation and make positive changes where needed.

Every one with good sense wants to learn, Prov. 18: 15, CEV.

In contrast the immature manager is defensive, resentful and hostile when his ideas and opinions are challenged. The immature manager allows disagreement to blossom into conflict. Disagreements can make us more tolerant of others views. Disagreements can be good teachers for change. One must learn to agree to disagree. Too many managers don't see criticism as a help, but a hindrance. Do not refuse to accept criticism. Get all the help you can.

Conflict and Serving.

Conflict provides an excellent opportunity to serve others. Jesus said,

If someone sues you for your shirt, give up your coat as well. If a soldier forces you to carry his pack one mile, carry it two miles, Matt. 5: 40-41, CEV.

Be sensitive to others needs. Be committed to resolving conflict quickly. Take the initiative in confronting those involved; don't wait for them to come to you. Even though anger is involved in conflict, avoid angry arguments. If we show our anger we stimulate anger in others. If we control our emotions during a confrontation, we ease the tension in others and it will be easier to come to a satisfactory solution.

It's smart to be patient, but it's stupid to lose your temper, Prov. 14: 29, CEV.

Conflict is inevitable in any organization. Remember that in conflict the emphasis is on self. Conflict always produces negative results for individuals and organizations. Keep in mind disagreements which lack hostility can be beneficial to organizations and individuals.

Chapter Ten

Working Relationships

Relationships with God and Men.

In the Bible we see described man's relationship with God and his relationship with other men. The Ten Commandments are an example. The first four commandments deal with man's relationship with God and the other six deal with his relationships with other men. Throughout the Bible we are reminded that these relationships must be good relationships.. The psalmist exclaimed,

> *It truly is wonderful when relatives get together in peace,* Ps. 133: 1, CEV.

Paul said;

> *My dear friends, as a follower of our Lord Jesus Christ, I beg you to get along with each other. Don't take sides. Always try to agree in what you think,* 1 Cor. 1: 10, CEV.

The Christian manager interested in applying Biblical management principles must work at developing and maintaining good working relationships with his people and organizations as well as with other people.

All management and leadership skills such as planning, organizing, leading, staffing and evaluating have good working relationships as their foundation. These management skills will be unproductive if the manager does not develop and maintain working relationships.

A Christian manager must apply the Bible's approach to people relationships. The lay management approach is to get people to meet one's needs. The Biblical approach is to meet the needs of others. Everyone has needs that can be met only by forming relationships with other people.

Adam lived alone in the Garden of Eden. He enjoyed a perfect spiritual relationship with his Maker. In Gen 2: 18, CEV the Lord said man should not live alone. This was not good. That did not surprise Adam because he knew the Lord knew that Adam had needs that could only be met with another person.

Failure of a manager to recognize the basic principle that people need other people has caused many mangers to develop serious relationship problems with others. People form relationships because they have needs that can be met by others. Needs that are met build relationships while unmet needs erode relationships.

Basic Styles of Relationships.

People relationships can be classified into four basic styles: Cooperation, Retaliation, Domination and Isolation. These relationships will usually develop over time with any group. The change from one to another is usually a gradual one.

Cooperation.

When a relationship begins it usually operates in a cooperation style. It is marked by the condition of mutual commitment to meet the other person's needs.

> *Don't be jealous or proud, but be humble and consider others more important than yourselves and think the same way Jesus Christ thought,* Phil. 2: 3-5, CEV.

We must stress meeting the needs of others and put more emphasis on others than self. The goal of the cooperation relationship is to serve people in meeting their needs through mutual trust and respect. People operating in the cooperation style experience harmony with the group. They enjoy each others company and rarely question motives. Mutual use of gifts, skills and creativity takes place. People never get a left out feeling because they are operating at a high level of cooperative participation.

There is joint development of solutions to problems and those affected by or involved in the solution should participate in problem solutions. The cooperation style is healthy and productive and tensions are at a minimum. As the group develops mutual trust and respect and the use of gifts and skills bring a feeling of accomplishment. The group has a strong commitment to the relationship.

Retaliation.

Eventually some in the group will think that in a particular instance it is important for their needs to be met rather than anyone else's needs to be met. This is the beginning of the retaliation style relationships. This style begins when selfishness overrides serving. The move to this style begins in a subtle, perhaps unnoticed manner. It comes into the open in the form of conflict.

The retaliation style attempts to make others confirm to what the manager wants. Then this style moves to aggressive actions towards others. Managers do this by using their position to pressure people to go along with their own wishes. The manager views others as objects not people with their own needs. The manager using the retaliation style rapidly begins to lose interest in the needs of others.

Domination.

The next move is a struggle for domination. The manager will develop an attitude of what is the best for me is the best for you. Once the struggle for domination begins, a period of conflict will occur. The manager assumes he can make sure his needs are met by controlling others. There will eventually be a winner and a loser. The retaliation and domination styles of relationships were condemned by Jesus.

> *You have been taught, an eye for an eye and a tooth for a tooth. But I tell you not to try to get even with a person that has done something to you When someone slaps your right cheek, turn and let that person slap the other cheek,* Matt. 5: 38-39, CEV.

Jesus is telling us when people take advantage of us and misuse us, do not stop serving them. Failure to serve others leads to a self-centered retaliation style relationship and eventually to a domination style of relationship. When a person succeeds with the struggle for control and moves on to a domination style, people are required to meet his needs. He rarely meets theirs. The loser is controlled by the winner. The winner becomes the decision-maker. Others in the group are required to give in to the wishes and ideas of the dominator.

As the domination style progresses, the dominator begins forcing others in the group to become what he wants them to be. The dominator wants to control how others act and think and will not accept ideas that are contrary to his own. People in a domination style group lose respect for one another.

Concern for another's needs continues to decrease. The dominator stops caring about the skills and creativity of those in the group. The manager ignores any idea or activity that does not promote him and his skills. Eventually those in the group attempt to manipulate the dominator to get their needs met. Eventually those in the group feel the situation is hopeless and stop trying to get their needs met. When this occurs, they take the first step toward the isolation style of relationships,

Isolation.

Communication breaks down. People become more withdrawn and isolated from each other. Mistrust increases in the group. Motives are questioned and hostility increases. Members of the group become more defensive and argumentative. The group becomes faced with problems they do not try to solve. Solutions offered are rejected.

Most needs of the people are unmet. Individuals cannot see how their self-centeredness is hurting others in the group.

Productivity of the group is greatly decreased. Usually, at this point the group is no longer functional and often the group is terminated. The isolation group is a very unhappy bunch of people.

Christian Approach to Relationships.

Christians often try to suppress their problems and not bring them out into the open to be dealt with and solved. Suppression of and resulting failure to deal with relationship problems indicates spiritual immaturity. The mature person faces problems and commits himself to finding a solution. Jesus said,

> So if you are about to place your sacrifice on the altar and remember that someone is angry with you, leave you gift there in front of the altar. Make peace with that person, then come back and offer your gift to God, Matt. 5: 23-24, CEV.

As soon as a relationship begins to move out of the cooperative style the following actions might be taken: Admit to yourself your current relationship style. Admit your faults to one another in the group. See Jms. 5: 16, CEV. This is a start in restoring cooperative relationships. It generally is easier to see others faults than your own faults. Jesus said,

> Don't condemn others, and God won't condemn you. God will be as

hard on you as you are on others!
He will treat you exactly as you
treat others, Matt. 7: 1-2, CEV.

Jesus makes it clear that we are to focus on our own mistakes and faults and not criticize others.

Admit that selfishness is a sin and ask God and others involved to forgive you. In Matt. 6: 14-17, CEV, we are told to forgive one another. This is the most important step in returning to the cooperation style of relationships. Asking for forgiveness is one of the most difficult things to do. In order to ask for forgiveness one must recognize his own faults. Make a decision to stay with the cooperation style of relationships and work at it.

Don't be jealous or proud, but be
humble and consider others more
important that yourself. Care about
them as much as you care about
yourself, Phil. 2: 3-4, CEV.

Begin acting out of love. In 1 Cor. 13: 4-8, CEV these verses define love in action and focus on others rather than self. You should be patient and kind, never jealous or envious, never boastful or proud, never haughty or selfish or rude. Start thanking God for those in the relationship. People are not always easy to get along with. It is possible when we are irritated by others it is a weakness of our character. James 1: 2-4, CEV tells us to be thankful during trials because they help perfect us. Some rules for harmonious cooperation are:

- Attack the problem, not the person.
- Verbalize feelings, don't act them out.
- Forgive in place of judging.
- Committ to give more than one takes.

Working relationships are important to most people. The people we work with on a daily basis are the people we spend the largest amount of our time with. It is very worthwhile for us to go out of our way to have good working relationships.

Chapter Eleven

Anger Hurt, Wound Shadow

Managers and Anger.

This chapter on anger is usually not found in management texts. This chapter applies to all persons reading this text. It definitely applies to Christian managers as well as lay managers. Managers have to concerned with anger in themselves as well as others. Handling anger as a manager is particularly difficult if the person you are angry at is a person who works for you. Although you can show your anger to that person, he may not be able to show his anger because of the boss/worker relationship.

Anger does not just occur. Behind that anger will be a hurt, a wound, or a shadow. Although a hurt does not always result in anger, it does quite frequently. A wound is more intense than a hurt and almost always results in some type of anger. A shadow is anger a person has had for a long time, though you repress it. At times a shadow will be held in your subconscious mind and you may not be aware of it until it surfaces.

Anger Defined.

Anger is generally defined as a strong feeling of hostility or indignation. It is a state of emotional excitement induced by a real or imagined threat, insult, put-down, frustration or injustice to yourself or to others. Anger brings about the fight or flight response. Anger may be camouflaged so that others are unaware of your anger. It can be denied to the extent that an individual can be unaware of his anger. With the outward showing of anger everyone is aware that a person is angry.

Conflict between people is normal and at times inevitable. However, we generally look upon anger as an abnormal state or as a sign of deficiency. It is simply a fact of life at times we will get angry at the people who are closest to us. This is part of the dynamics of people who live close to each other. We need to come to the acceptance that anger is normal and that it is inevitable.

Misconceptions About Anger.

Most people have misconceptions about anger. They believe if one doesn't look, feel or seem angry, one does not have an anger problem. Squelching our anger never pays. Suppressed anger has a way of coming out. Sometimes it just bursts forth. When that happens, someone is likely to get hurt. Many people have the idea that if they ignore anger it will go away and won't cause any problems. This is contrasted with the misconception that if you let all your feelings out of your system, you will solve all of your anger problems.

One thought many Christians rely on is that it won't cost me too much emotionally to be a nice person who never shows anger with anyone. This is tied to the misconception that if I express my anger to the person I'm angry at, our relationship will suffer. It may or may not.

How We Hide Our Anger.

We can camouflage our anger by following the peace-at-any-price methodology. Some people can cope with each little hurt. But they save up every little grievance, annoyance or irritation. Sometimes these people are thought of as martyrs, then one day they boil over. The last incident may be minor, but the accumulation of anger comes out as pent-up rage.

Another way we camouflage anger is by using the silent approach. A person will retreat into silence. When asked if anything is bothering you, you will deny it. We can also camouflage anger by criticizing and being sarcastic about everything. Usually we sense something is wrong from the undertone of anger and hostility.

Another type of behavior is being passive-aggressive. The aggressive behavior is shown in passive ways, like pouting, stubbornness and procrastination. This type person will almost always take the opposite of any opinion being expressed. The next day he can take the opposite point of view from the day before. Prolonged contact with this type of person is very difficult and can be extremely frustrating.

People who think anger is wrong can actually convince themselves there is no anger in their lives. This usually occurs at the subconscious level in their minds and they are often unaware of this. The anger does not go away it just accumulates. This pent up anger can show itself physically in psychosomatic illnesses.

We have touched on camouflaged and denied anger. We can also have a person who is the opposite. He is overtly angry most of the time and shows it. Our goal should be to handle our anger in a constructive way.

What The Bible Says About Anger.

When we attempt to take a constructive approach to anger, are we then saying that anger is all right? Some verses in the Bible say anger is wrong.

Stop being bitter and angry and mad at others, Eph. 4: 31, CEV.

Don't be angry or furious. Anger can lead to sin, Ps. 37: 8, CEV.

But I promise you that if you are angry with someone, you will have to stand trial, Matt. 5: 22, CEV.

In contrast some parts of the Bible seem to condone anger.

Don't get so angry that you sin. Eph. 4: 26, CEV.

Many of the men in the Bible showed anger. Study of the Bible shows that many of the men did get angry, which is contrary to the stereotypes many Christians have of these men today..

Moses became very angry when he came down from the mountain and discovered the Israelites had started worshiping idols. He was so angry that he smashed the stone tablets upon which the law had been written. See Ex. 12: 19, CEV.

David was described as a man after God's own heart. See Acts 13: 22, CEV. Yet he became angry with God when a man was killed trying to protect the ark of God. See 2 Sam. 6: 6-8, CEV.

We might argue that the men of the Bible were sinning when they got angry. Yet there are two people in the Bible we cannot accuse of sinning when they got angry. Are you aware of who in the Bible got angry the most often? It was God himself. If God who is without sin shows anger cannot man show anger?

The Hebrew word for anger appears approximately 455 times in the Old Testament, and 375 times it is referring to the anger of God. Contrary to the image we have of him as a quiet, peaceful soul, Jesus became angry at times.

He got angry when He saw the callous attitudes of the people as He was about to heal the man with a paralyzed hand See Mark 3: 1-5, CEV. Again we see Jesus being angry when He is driving out the parasitic money changers in the temple with a whip, shouting after them See Mark 11: 15-17, CEV.

There are other times in the New Testament where Jesus' anger is described.

The Use of Hebrew and Greek Words for Anger.

How can we reconcile one verse where God is angry with another verse where God tells us not to be angry? Perhaps it might be in the interpretation of the Hebrew word for anger. The Hebrew word most frequently translated as anger comes from the word aph. This word appears several hundred times in the Hebrew

Old Testament. It usually describes God's obviously appropriate anger.

> One day the Israelites started complaining about their troubles. The Lord heard them and became so angry that he destroyed the outer edges of their camp with fire, Num. 11: 1. CEV.

This word aph describes Moses' strong but questionable emotions when he smashed the stone tablets of the law.

In the New Testament, the Greek word orge is translated as anger. This word is sometimes used to describe appropriate anger, such as God's or Christ's See Heb. 3: 11, Rom. 9: 22, Mark 3: 5, CEV.

> Stop being bitter and angry with others. Don't yell at One another or ever be rude. Instead be kind and merciful, and forgive others, just as God forgave you because of Christ, Eph. 4:31, CEV.

> My dear friends, you should be quick to listen, slow to speak or to get angry, James 1: 19, CEV.

The word orge was used to describe both appropriate and inappropriate anger.

Another Greek word orgizo means to be angry. See Matt. 5: 22, Eph. 4: 26, CEV. Each of the words which translated anger is used in positive, negative and neutral meanings. We must look to the context of each verse to see if anger is justified.. It is the same with our own lives. We must look at the context to see if our anger is justified.. What the anger is based on and how the anger is expressed determines whether it is right or wrong. In the study of psychology we find that anger is basically neutral but may have an appropriate or inappropriate basis.

The Bible offers many ways for handling anger properly. It should be understood that feelings of anger as well as emotions of all kinds, are God given gifts. God in his wisdom created us in his own image, and one of the things he created was the ability for us to get angry. See Gen. 1: 26-27, CEV. Feelings can be used to serve us and to serve God. To deny feelings is to deny a part of the person God created us to be.

How to Handle Anger Constructively.

A person can handle only so much hurt, wounds, shadows, repressed feelings, and conflict, If we internalize this hurt and anger, eventually it will find a way out. Bringing conflict out into the open and dealing with it constructively can be called confrontation. But many people try to avoid confrontation at all costs. The idea of dealing with their own feelings or someone else's feelings in a constructive direct way is very uncomfortable for them. Dealing with anger constructively is to many people more uncomfortable than dealing with it destructively.

Many people have been taught that standing up to others is wrong. People may get so much praise for being a nice person that they find it hard to tarnish that image. Most people do not fully grasp the long term consequences of failing to confront those with whom they are angry. They will continue to be angry and keep it camouflaged. This condition in the long run can harm you both physically and mentally.

Anger can be a very valuable force if we put it to constructive use. It can be a positive motivation in our lives. People can handle constructively expressed anger much better than repressed or camouflaged anger. If a relationship is destroyed by attempting to deal with it constructively when one is angry, the relationship was probably not a good one to begin with. Confronting another person should not be looked upon as a sign of hostility. Rather it shows that you care enough about the person to work out the problem in the relationship.

Ways to Handle Anger.

The first step is to recognize and get in touch with your feelings of hurt, wound or shadow. At this point do not judge these feelings as to whether they are reasonable or not, or even whether they are right or wrong. Try to determine if you are a little upset, moderately upset or very upset. This will serve as a valuable clue as to the actions you need to take.

The second step is to suppress taking any action until you have thought through the situation and have control of what you are going to say or do. The Bible tells us not to be hasty in responding to our anger.

Don't be a fool and quickly lose your temper but be sensible and patient, Prov. 29:11, CEV.

Though one should not take any action at this time, there is an exception. If someone asks you if you are upset, you will be tempted to say that it did not bother me. If you were bothered it would be dishonest. It would be better to say that you are upset, but you will have to think about it.

The third step is to pray, particularly in very stressful situations. Prayer can be short and to the point. An example would be, "Lord help me to see the issues in this situation more clearly." Or perhaps, "Lord please help me to sort out my feelings so I can do the right thing." You do not have to pray in every instance, but prayer should come from the desire of the heart.

The fourth step is to identify the cause of your anger. What is the primary feeling that is leading to your anger feelings? What is threatened? Often the cause of our anger is obvious. However, you may have difficulty with this step of figuring out what made you angry. You will develop your own way to determine the events that led to the anger. You may want to put it on paper. Or to talk it over with a close friend. You may have to have help to identify the source of your anger. Keep in mind that there is often more than one issue you may have to deal with.

The fifth step is to determine if the anger is legitimate?

> *Nehemiah said, When I heard their complaints and charges I became very angry, so I thought it over and said to the leaders and officials, how can you charge your own people interest?* Neh. 5: 6-7, CEV.

In this passage Nehemiah was angry because his fellow Jews were charging interest to their brethren who wanted the money to buy their sons and daughters out of slavery. Nehemiah was able to get in touch with his feelings, think it through and then take appropriate action.

One way you could look at the situation is to ask yourself the question of whether or not is this event worth getting upset and angry?

> But the Lord asked Jonah, do you have the right to be angry about the vine? Yes I do Jonah answered, and I am angry enough to die Jon. 4: 9, CEV.

As it turned out Jonah did not have just cause for his anger. If the situation has been resolved at any one step, the step that follows will not be necessary.

The sixth step is concerned with the situation that is not resolved. One will have to determine a course of action. You will have to find a way to deal with your feelings constructively. If you do not, your feelings will turn into a destructive force. Most people deal with conflict by angrily attacking, running away, withdrawing or giving in to the other person.

You may be in total denial that there is no conflict. This only magnifies the situation and makes handling the conflict very difficult. The methods listed above are just a few methods of dealing with conflict, although many people rely on these methods. There is a large array of skills that one can use to resolve conflict. One needs to become proficient with all these skills.

Confrontation

The skill that will probably work best is to confront the person with whom you are having the conflict. People who care about others often find confrontation difficult. A mature person will confront someone when it is needed. Paul shared with how he felt about confrontation.

> *At the time I wrote I was suffering terribly. My eyes were full of tears, and my heart was broken. But I didn't want you to feel bad. I only wanted to let you know how much I cared for you,* 2 Cor. 2: 4, CEV.

- When you find confrontation a necessity use the following steps.
- What is the issue?
- Be very specific; don't generalize.
- What do both of you agree on?
- Be specific on what you need.
- Make a list. Put it in writing.
- Have accountability with each other.

It is important to remember the quoted verses about anger.

> *We are part of the same body. Stop lying and start telling each other the truth. Don't get so angry*

that you sin. Don't go to bed angry,
Eph. 4: 25-27, CEV.

Another way to put this is tell no falsehood, speak the truth, and be honest with each other. Paul states that one can be angry, but should not sin. Speaking the truth in love sometimes requires confrontation. This must happen before you can be tender and forgiving.

There are many examples of confrontation in the Bible. One example is when Jesus sharply attacked and confronted the Pharisees. See Mark 7, CEV. Jesus disciples could not understand His remarks to the religious leaders. On one occasion the religious leaders came to Him and He insulted the Pharisees. See Matt. 15: 12, CEV). Jesus did not retract His comments to the Pharisees because He had fully intended to confront them.

Confrontation is not necessarily a hostile, painful experience. It can be done in a tender and forgiving manner. An example of this is how Jesus treated the adulterous woman whom the Pharisees wanted to stone to death.

Jesus told the Pharisees, If any of you have never sinned, then go ahead and throw the first stone at her, John 8: 7, CEV.

Genuine confrontation, treating it with love, is not attacking another person, but caring enough about that person and the relationship to talk directly to him.

Whenever possible, it is best if the confrontation can be in private.

> *If one of My followers sins against you, go and point out what was wrong. But do it in private, just between the two of you,* Matt. 18: 15, CEV.

There are some exceptions to this position of having confrontation in private. If others have observed the conflict or were in some way involved in the conflict, it may need to be resolved with all the individuals present. Confrontation can vary widely from a gentle, private resolution of an issue, to a strong, possibly unpleasant situation involving others.

Ways to Confront People.

There are three general ways to confront people.

- First is to inform.
- Second is to share your primary feelings.
- Third is to rebuke in love.

When we feel something strongly, it is up to us to express it. We are asking for all kinds of trouble if you assume that the other person knows how we feel. We must actually put it into words and express our feelings directly to the person involved. A way to confront is to convey your feelings. The anger one feels is secondary to some insult, threat, put-down or frustration.

The initial primary feeling is hurt. If it is important to you and it is not resolved it may become a wound. If it is very traumatic or not resolved and goes on for a long time it can become a shadow. Shadows that we carry through life as baggage are very difficult to resolve.

You might consider sending an I feel message. This type of message is a good way of sharing how one feels and helps everyone involved get in touch with their feelings. Compare the following I feel messages as compared to the blaming you messages.

- I'm feeling ignored.
- You are making me mad because you are paying so much attention to everyone else.
- I get the feeling that I am being blamed.
- You always blame me for everything that goes wrong.
- I feel you do not listen to me.
- You never hear a word I say and it is your fault.
- I feel like I am being questioned.
- Why are you finding fault with me again?
- I feel put down.

- You are always putting me down.

In contrast to the I feel messages blaming you messages usually have the word you in them. They accuse the other person quite frequently. Blaming you messages are usually hard to defend. They tend to raise hostilities and defenses by the other person. They are often judgmental, critical and attack the other person.

The strongest manner to confront someone is to rebuke with love. With this method, you are telling the person what he is saying or doing is not right. Since this is done with love, it is different from an angry attack.

A truly good friend will openly correct you. You can trust a friend who corrects you, but kisses from an enemy are nothing but lies, Prov.27: 5-6, CEV.

Setting Limits of Behavior.

As a manager you can establish limits of behavior. Limits can be set with predetermined consequences. Everyone must be informed of what those predetermined consequences are. Setting limits is applicable to parents and teachers as well as managers. When setting limits the rules and regulations must be fair and consistently applied. When the limits are set you must follow through on the consequences for breaking the limits. There will be a temptation to make just one exception. It is not a good idea to set the consequence after the offense has been committed.

Seek Counsel.

Another way you can handle negative feelings, hurts, wounds or shadows is to seek counsel. All of us at one time or another find ourselves in need of someone with whom we can talk about a problem. This does not always have to be a professional counselor but can be a friend, a spouse or peer who can help you to clarify the issues. This person should be mature, be a good listener and should not be quick to give answers. He should be a person who will not gossip about your problem or use it against you.

There are a growing number of groups that could be labeled support groups for men and women either together or separate. After the group has formed there develops an environment of trust. You feel you can talk in this group without fear of what one says being repeated outside the group.

There are also a growing number of organizations you can attend, usually for a weekend. During this weekend you will have the opportunity to work on your shadows and you usually will be involved in psychodrama. This is particularly good to identify and work through your shadows that have been repressed for a long time, even years. Almost all of these psychodrama groups have follow up methods whereby you can continue to work on your shadows. Without follow on work you may slip back into your shadow which you do not want to do. Be sure the organization has some type of follow on work.

Catharsis..

Catharsis is a term that means to cleanse or purge, to talk things out. It is a healthy release of ideas and feelings, especially the painful ones. This has to be done in an environment where one can trust the people without reservation. Prayer can aid catharsis. Some people can share their deepest feelings with God. Often catharsis is all that is needed to dissipate one's anger.

Compromise.

Compromise is a viable option. It is rare when we are 100% right and the other person is 100% wrong. Quite frequently there are multiple factors involved with the situation. There can be different ways to look at and interpret the situation. In the process of trying to handle our anger, we become aware of the other person's feelings. A characteristic of the emotionally mature person is the ability to compromise.. Compromise is a gift to human relationships.

Forgive and Forget

At times we must learn to let an issue go. This is not camouflaging the issues. The reason for letting go of an issue is realizing it is the best solution for all involved. It means that we bear no grudges, that we are willing to forgive and forget. You cannot make me angry unless I choose to be angry. You also cannot discourage or disgust me unless I choose to be so.

If you are going to let an issue go, you must have an awareness of the injury done to us. We also must have a deliberate willingness to completely drop the anger with the person who has hurt us. We may decide it is not worth it to us and the other person to press on.

> *It is wise to be patient and show what you are like by forgiving others,* Prov. 19: 11, CEV.

The final and most difficult step in dealing with anger and the most crucial one is to forgive and forget.

> *If you don't forgive others, your Father will not forgive your sins,* Matt. 6: 15, CEV.

Many people have misunderstandings about what forgiveness really is. Many of us when trying to forgive someone, try to talk ourselves into thinking what the other person did was not really wrong; he did not mean to do it, or we overreacted to what he did. This may be true, but at times we need to fully recognize that what he did was wrong, and we must forgive him and forget it, no matter how much we have been hurt. Forgiveness means we choose to forgive and give up our grudge against a person.

Some things really hurt, but after recognizing that hurt, we choose to forgive. Forgiving does not mean that the party at fault does not need to suffer the consequences of his actions. One can forgive and allow justice to be administered. Often we come to the forgiveness step after we have taken some of the previous steps. No matter how many of the steps we have taken, if we don't forgive that person and try to forget there are going to be repercussions in our own lives.

Summation.

There are four paths people commonly take when angry. These four paths are to attack, run, give in and deny the situation. These paths are basically destructive reactions to anger. These paths in the long run only add to our problems. The constructive ways in dealing with anger are as follows.

- To recognize our feelings and determine how upset we are.

- To suppress taking action until we have control of our words and actions.

- Use prayer as a help in controlling anger.
- Does our anger have a legitimate basis?
- Confront and use I feel messages.
- Rebuke with love.
- Establish limits with consequences.
- Get counsel or join a support group.
- Use catharsis.
- Learn how to compromise.
- Pass over the issue.
- Forgive and forget.
- Have resolution of your anger.

Although we have put in a step for prayer, if it is the desire of your heart, you can pray with each step. Never forget the power of prayer.

Today, Lord, cast out of
my mind all my destructive
negative thinking.
Help me to tear down my
shrines of cynicism and'
emotional doubts.
Teach me to believe that
all things are possible
if only I believe.
Amen

EPILOGUE

Help each other in a sharing way.

God's spirit makes us loving, happy, peaceful, kind, good, faithful, gentle and self-controlled, Gal. 5: 22-23, CEV.

All of us who are mature should think in this same way. and if any of you think differently, God will make it clear to you, Phil. 3:15, CEV.

Have an attitude of success. Use persistence and hang in there until you have accomplished what you set out to do. Have positive self-awareness that is based on the truth. Live a life where you worry only about the things that can be changed. Do not worry about the things that cannot be changed. Live your life without limits. Most important, understand and use the power of prayer! Go to the Bible routinely and in time of need.

Then you will live a life that honors the Lord, and you will always please him by doing good deeds. You will come to know God even better, Col 1: 10.

I leave you with some concepts that may help guide you to be a success as a Christian manager.

~ Have a vision for your life.

~ Develop a plan for your life and with this plan develop strategies to make things happen.

~ Always live with the truth and learn to be flexible.

~ Learn what the risks are and do not shy from any risks that can be overcome.

~ Set priorities in your life and take action when it is needed.

~ Live your life and what you do with passion.

~ As a Christian manager learn to serve those you work with.

~ Above all else know thyself.

I close this handbook with the same words with which I started.

The Love We Hold Back
Is
The Pain We Live With!

Ora B. Clark, 1951

Appendix One

Christian Management Topics

All Bible References are Contemporary English Version Bible.

Accountability	2 Cor. 8:21
Adversity	Ecc. 7: 14
Anxiety	Phil. 4: 6-7
Authority	Mark 10: 42-45
Competition	1 Cor. 9: 24-27
Confidence	Phil. 4: 13
Confrontation	Prov. 28: 23
Conscience	Acts 24: 6
Contentment	1 Tim. 6: 6
Counsel	Prov. 1; 5
Decision Making	1 Kings 18:21
Diligence	Ecc. 11: 6
Employees	Col. 3: 22-25
Excellence	Col. 3: 12
Failure	Matt. 7: 24-27
Faith	Mark 9: 23
Fear	2 Tim. 1: 7
Forgiveness	Eph. 4: 31-32

Generosity	Prov. 11: 24
Giving	Luke 6: 38
Goals	Phil. 3: 12-14
Influence	Matt. 5: 13-16
Initiative	Prov. 6: 6-8
Integrity	Psalm 15
Leadership	Matt. 20: 25-28
Loyalty	Prov. 27: 18
Meditation	Josh. 1: 28
Money	Luke :16: 10
Patience	James 1: 3
Peace	Phil. 4: 6
Persecution	Matt. 5: 44
Planning	Prov. 16: 9
Priorities	Matt. 6: 33
Procrastination	John 8: 32
Promotion	Psalm 75: 6-7R
Reconciliation	Matt. 5: 24
Rejection	Matt. 21: 42
Relationships	Matt. 22: 37-39
Rewards	Col. 3: 24
Security	Josh. 1: 9
Sowing, Reaping	Gal. 6: 7
Stress	James 1: 2-4

Success	Matt. 25: 21
Temptation	1 Cor. 10: 13
Time	James 4: 13
The Tongue	Prov. 18: 21-22
Wealth	1 Tim. 6: 17-19
Wisdom	James 1: 5
Work	Ecc. 5: 18-20
Worth	Eph. 3: 6

Appendix Two

Thoughts To Help Christian Managers

Some persons see things as they are and ask, "Why"? Christian Managers dream of things that have not been and ask, "Why not"?

Apologies are what keeps relationships stable. An apology sincerely given can make things right.

Be kind to people, they are fighting to do things right, just as you are.

By being interested you can make friends readily. Much easier than getting them interested in you.

How ever many times you fall get up one more time.

If you want to be thought of as wise, know what to overlook.

You can't base your life on what others think of you.

What is success? There are two ways to judge success, from our viewpoint and from the viewpoint of others. A successful life does not require that we have done the best, but that we have done our best with self-discipline, integrity, kindness and courage. These are still the secrets to successful living.

There are always people who will come up with reasons why you can't do what you want to do, ignore them!!

It is OK to admit you can't do everything.

People should have the freedom to do things their own way and express their individuality so long as the job gets done.

Stand up for yourself.

Past performance does not always dictate future results.

Learn what a work ethic is about and follow it.

If you make a commitment, keep it.

Don't let little things get in the way of the big picture.

Learn how to say no.

Accept reality.

Rely on God given intuition, Know the value of intuition.

Show confidence.

Offer assistance.

Avoid saying "but" when turning an employees idea down.

Tell the truth.

Listen to your people.

Stay humble

Do your homework.

Have fun doing your work..

Appendix Three

References

For Servant Leadership

Autry, James A.; "The Servant Leader; How to Build a Creative Team, Develop Great Morale and Improve Bottom Line Performance"; Prima Publishing, Roseville CA ; 2001.

Harry and Richard Blackeby; "Spiritual Leadership; Moving People on God's Agenda"; Broodman and Holman Publishers, Nashville; 1995.

Ken Blanchard and Phil Hodges; "The Servant Leader; Transforming your Heart, Head, Hands and Habits"; J. Countryman, A Division of Thomas Nelson, Inc., Nashville; 2003.

Greenleaf, Robert 'The Servant as Leader"; The Robert K. Greenleaf Center, Indianapolis, IN: 1991.

James C. Hunter: "*A Simple Story* The Servant; A Simple Story About the True Essence of Leadership"; Prima Publishing, Roseville, CA; 1998

Edited by Larry Spears: "Essays on Reflections on Leadership: How Robert Greenleaf's

Theory of Servant Leadership Influenced Today's Top Management Thinkers"; John Wiley and Sons, New York; 1995

For Secular Management

Ackerman, Laurence D.:"Identity Is Destny"; Berrett-Kohler, San Francisco, 2000

Brache, Alan P. "How Organizations Work", John Wiley & Sons, New York, 2002

Dortch, Thomas W.:"The Miracle of Mentoring"; Doubleday, New York, 2000

Drucker, Peter F.: "Management, Tasks, Responsibilities, Practices"; Harper and Row, Publishers, New York 1974

Drucker, Peter F.:"People and Performance; The Best of Peter Drucker on Management"; Harper and Row, Publishers, New York 1977

Drucker, Peter F.:"The Age of Discontinuity; Guidelines to our Changing Society"; Harper and Row, Publishers, New York 1969

Gutek, Barbara A. and Welsh, Theresa: "The Brave New Service Strategy"; AMA-Com, New York, 2000

Ivanovich, John M. and Matteson, Michael T.: "Organizational Behavior and Management"; BPI Irwin, Homewood, IL 1990

Katzenbach, Jon R: "Why Pride Matters More Than Money"; Crown Business, 2002

Kotter, R. John and Cohen, Dan: "The Heart of Change"; Harvard Business School Press, Boston, 2002

McKenna, Patrick J. and Maister, David H.: "First Among Equals"; The Free Press, Simon & Schuster, New York, 2002

Nutt, Paul C.: "Why Decisions Fail"; Berett – Kohler, San Francisco, 2002

Okun, Barbara F.:"Effective Helping, Interviewing and Counseling Techniques", Third Edition; Brooks/Cole Publishing Company, Monterey, CA, 1976

Harris, Dean M.:"Healthcare Law and Ethics"; Health Administration Press, Chicago, AUPHA Press, Washington, DC, 1999

Lipmann. Walter: "A Preface to Morals"; Time-Life Books, New York,1957

Smith, Preston G. and Merritt, Guy M.: "Proactive Risk Management"; Productivity Press, New York, 2002

Sternberg, Robert J., et al: "Practical Intelligence in Everyday Life"; Cambridge University Press, Cambridge, UK, 2000

Sternberg, Robert J.: "Successful Intelligence: How Practical and Creative Intelligence

Determine Success in Life"; Simon & Schuster, New York, 2002

For Christian Managers

Anderson, Ken: "Where To Find It In The Bible"; Thomas Nelson, Inc, Nashville 1996

Burkett, Larry: "Business by the Book"; Thomas Nelson Publishers, Nashville, 1997

Gills, James P., MD: "Come Unto Me"; Trinity College, Holiday, FL, 1988

"Holy Bible, Contemporary English Version"; American Bible Society; New York, 1995

Jones, Laurie Beth: "Jesus CEO, Using Ancient Wisdom for Visionary Leadership"; Hyperon Publishers; New York, 1996

LaHaye, Tim: "Revelation Unveiled"; Zondervan, Grand Rapids, MI, 1999

Milne, Bruce: "Know the Truth, A Handbook of Christian Belief"; Inner Varsity Press, Downers Grove, IL, 1982

Radmacher, Earl D., ThD, General Editor: "The Nelson Study Bible", NKJ; Thomas Nelson Publishers, Nashville, 1997

Stanley, Charles: "Priority Profiles for Today"; Thomas Nelson Publishers, Nashville, 1998

Strong, James, LLD, STD: "Strong's Complete Dictionary of Bible Words"; Thomas Nelson Publishers, Nashville, 1996

Wright, H. Norman: "How To Get Along With Almost Anyone; A Complete Guide to Building Positive Relationships with Family, Friends, Co-Workers"; Word Publishing, 1989";

Yancy, Phillip: "Where is God When it Hurts"; Harper Collins Publishers, 1977

Other References

Bly, Robert: "A Little Book On The Human Shadow"; Harper, San Francisco, 1988

Warlick, Harold C.: "Conquering Loneliness"; Word Incorporated, Waco, TX, 1979